WITH MOUNTED INFANTRY IN TIBET

WITH MOUNTED INFANTRY IN TIBET

BY

BREVET-MAJOR W.J. OTTLEY

GYAN

Published by

GYAN

Gyan Publishing House
5, Ansari Road
Daryaganj, New Delhi-110002
Phone: 011-47034999, 9811692060
E-mail: books@gyanbooks.com

Distribution Network
gyanbooks.com
India, USA, Canada, UK, Australia

ISBN: 978-93-6433-541-6 (HB)
First Published, 1906

2nd Impression 2024

Printed at: Gyan Press, Delhi.

WITH MOUNTED INFANTRY IN TIBET
Author: BREVET-MAJOR W.J. OTTLEY

WITH MOUNTED INFANTRY IN TIBET

Photo by ELLIOTT & FRY.]

BRIGADIER-GENERAL SIR J. R. L. MACDONALD,
K.C.I.E., C.B., R.E.

WITH MOUNTED INFANTRY IN TIBET

BY

BREVET-MAJOR W. J. OTTLEY

34TH SIKH PIONEERS

WITH PORTRAITS, ILLUSTRATIONS AND PLAN

LONDON

SMITH, ELDER, & CO., 15 WATERLOO PLACE

1906

THIS BOOK IS DEDICATED

TO THE

23RD AND 32ND SIKH PIONEERS

AND THE

8TH GURKHA RIFLES

IN A SPIRIT OF GRATEFULNESS FOR THE

SELECTION AND CHOICE OF THE NON-COMMISSIONED OFFICERS

AND MEN DETAILED FROM EACH REGIMENT

FOR SERVICE WITH MOUNTED INFANTRY IN TIBET

PREFACE

On the demobilisation of the Tibet Mission Force some officers of the Sikh Pioneer and Gurkha Regiments suggested to me that I should write an account of the doings of the native officers and men who composed the 1st Company of Mounted Infantry in the Tibet Mission Force, as they considered it would be interesting to the regiments of those races in the Indian Army, and would commemorate the first occasion that Native Mounted Infantry have been employed on active service on or beyond the Indian frontier in Asia.

The 32nd Sikh Pioneers were raised during the great Indian Mutiny, and were employed at Delhi in fortifying and defending the British camp at that memorable siege. A detachment of them carried and laid the powder-bags to blow in the Cashmir Gate, which led to the fall of the city. The whole detachment (nineteen men) were either killed or wounded.

The 23rd Sikh Pioneers were raised immediately

after the Mutiny, and since then both these regiments have been employed on every kind of military duty—as pioneers, engineers, infantry soldiers, artillerymen—and now they have added one more branch of the Service to their long list of experiences, and have proved themselves as good mounted infantrymen as they are pioneers.

The Gurkha, of whom it has often been said that he would never become a success in the mounted branches of the Service, owing to his short stature and round legs, left nothing to be desired in his proficiency as an equestrian. The fact of several Gurkhas having ridden in the Lhasa races, some of which they won, shows that with training and practice they can become as good riders and mounted infantry as they are hardy and gallant foot soldiers.

I am indebted to Lieutenant Bailey for some of the photographs, and to Captain Stanley Clarke for the hand sketch, which he produced from a rough topographical sketch without having seen the ground.

W. J. O.

CONTENTS

APPENDICES

LIST OF ILLUSTRATIONS

WITH MOUNTED INFANTRY IN TIBET

CHAPTER I

THE RAISING OF THE 1ST MOUNTED INFANTRY

EVER since the introduction of mounted infantry in the Indian Army it has been a sore point with the three Sikh Pioneer regiments that the regulations do not permit them to send some of their British officers and men to be trained at the mounted infantry schools, like all other native infantry regiments. When a certain commanding officer of a Pioneer regiment applied for permission to do so, he was told that the authorities did not consider it necessary to train Pioneers as mounted infantry, but that every opportunity should be taken to train men of Pioneer regiments to ride in carts. As Pioneer regiments are chiefly employed in campaigns on the hilly frontiers of India, where carts cannot work, it appears that the high Staff officer who gave the above reply had some hidden joke in his mind.

It was fortunate for the 23rd and 32nd Sikh

Pioneers that General Macdonald was of a different opinion. He wanted mounted infantry on the spot when he advanced into the Chumbi Valley in December 1903, but as he then had only three regiments in the Tibet Mission Force—viz., the 23rd and 32nd Sikh Pioneers and the 8th Gurkha Rifles—he made up his mind to form some mounted infantry out of those three regiments, whether the men were trained or not. Now, the 8th Gurkhas had twenty-three men and one native officer of the 9th Gurkhas (attached), so that they were able to supply a complete section of mounted infantry. But alas for the training! Sepoys soon forget unless they are kept constantly in practice. Such was the case with the men of the 8th, who had been trained a year before. Nevertheless, they soon made up their lost ground, and, as will be seen, did splendid work. To the 23rd Pioneers, however, it was a surprise as pleasant as it was complete when, at Gnatong, the frontier town of Sikkim, nearly 15,000 feet above the sea, in thirty degrees of frost and a foot of snow, on December 7, General Macdonald's fiat went forth calling for thirty men from the 23rd and twenty men from the 8th Gurkhas for mounted infantry. First we merely received saddles and bridles; then the men were picked out. Meantime we were kept in darkness as to what the mounted infantry were to be mounted on. Every sort and kind of animal was suggested;

but at last some wag declared that he had solved the question for good and all : the mounted infantry were to be mounted on yaks, thousands of which were being collected on the Nepaul-Sikkim frontier to launch the Tibet Mission and Force into the forbidden land of Tibet. The author of this suggestion gravely added that fifty selected yaks were being sent up to Gnatong by double marches, but as they did not arrive on the date given by the humorist they were alleged to have died of heat when crossing the Teesta Valley in Sikkim; for although the country was full 7,000 feet above the sea, yet it was too hot for a yak.

To the regulation mentioned at the beginning of the chapter I had the luck to be an exception, thanks to General Sir Charles Egerton, commanding in the Punjab, who in 1901, when my regiment was on the Waziristan Blockade, was kind enough to direct that I should be trained at a mounted infantry school on the first opportunity. As we were on service, the opportunity did not arise till March 1903, when I was sent to the mounted infantry school at Sialkote for a three-months' course, the pleasantest course I have ever been through. Being the only qualified officer in the 23rd, I was given the thirty men of the regiment to train.

We started doing foot drill. This the men very soon picked up, but when they got their saddles and bridles all in little pieces tied up in a bag, the Sikhs were really in their glory. First they were mightily pleased that they were really going to be horse-soldiers; next, the saddlery was to them like a new toy to a child. It was full of wonders, especially the putting of it all together, and although I put one set together for them and told them to do the same, I found on my return about four hours afterwards the most extraordinary combinations of parts. Girths were supposed to be reins, and stirrup-leathers girths; cruppers were converted into standing martingales, and minor straps were left on the ground, while their owners patiently examined them and debated the proper point of attachment to saddles or bridles. Once these were all set right a great desire seized everybody to put them on something. The Maxim-gun mules were noticed standing very happily eating their food. The very thing! what could be better? So they were pulled out and the saddles put on, to an accompaniment of many and well-directed kicks delivered at the Sepoys, who took them manfully, and only retaliated in terms of endearment, calling the mules their very own brothers. The saddling-up took some time, and was not without amusing incidents. Some put the saddles on with the pummels facing the animal's tail; others passed the girths through the forelegs, and loud were the lamentations when these were found too short to buckle at the other side. One man distinguished himself by putting the bridle-reins in the mule's mouth, with the full intention of holding on to the bit when he mounted.

We had reached this stage at about 4 P.M. on December 10, when word came that the force would march next morning at 9 A.M. over the great frontier pass of the Jelap Là into Tibet, and that there might be a fight at Yatung, on the other side of the pass. These orders stimulated everybody to renewed efforts in their preparations to get under way. All being ready, the men were directed to mount. Anybody who was present as an onlooker at this performance will never forget it. Several Sepoys mounted most resolutely, but arrived in the saddle with their faces towards the tail instead of the head of the mule. The most amusing point was their own puzzled look at finding themselves in that situation, and their helpless endeavours to get into the right position, try as they would, till they were shown the way. Moreover, the saddlery had been made for animals of between fifteen and sixteen hands, so that it was much too large for the humble mule. This fact was demonstrated wonderfully well on the order to mount being given; for, as soon as a man put his ammunition-boot-shod foot in the stirrup, the girths, being too long to tighten properly, twisted round under the mule's stomach, man performed marvels of gymnastics underneath mule, and mule replied, after his custom, with vigorous kicking. In addition to these contretemps, mules have a way of herding together like sheep, and pushing and shoving against one another in seemingly aimless manner until they get rid of their loads, and often their saddles. The Sepoys had not bargained for this manœuvre, and several dropped to mother earth. Other mules, being of an enterprising spirit, took charge of their riders, and galloped off wildly till mule and rider alike ended up with a graceful header into a snowdrift.

It was 8 P.M. and bright moonlight when this exciting parade was over, and still we did not know what animals we were to start off on next morning. The only consolation I could give the men was that they would most probably have to ride yaks. Their reply was characteristic of Sikhs—' Baishuck, Sahib ka kushi hogea,' which really meant, ' We are quite ready to ride anything the Sahib pleases.' Later on the question of mounts was decided by orders that we should take over thirty and the Gurkhas twenty ponies from the Tibet Pony Transport Corps next morning before the march. At the same time we were told that, owing to shortness of transport, these ponies would be required to carry their usual two maunds (160 pounds) of rations, together with their saddles and bridles and transport equipment, as far as Chumbi, so that the men had to walk instead of riding, as they had expected. It did not matter; they were so pleased at being even called Mounted Infantry that they would have carried the sacks of rations themselves at the slightest hint to do so.

Thus ended the 10th of December, every man in the force in the best of spirits, in spite of the height, the frost, and the snow; every man filled with an ardent desire to get over the Jelap Là, snow or no snow, enemy or no enemy, into Tibet. But a bitter disappointment was in store for me and the double company of the 23rd which I commanded. About 11 P.M. I was summoned by my colonel, who told me that my double company had to stay behind, and that the Mounted Infantry men were to be handed over to Lieutenant Crosleigh of the regiment.

Everybody was afoot at 3 A.M. next day, the 11th, notwithstanding the cold—a damp cold which made one and all truly miserable. Indeed, but for the liberal supply of warm clothing, consisting of poshteens (sheepskin coats), trousers wadded with cotton-wool two inches thick, thick woollen vests, woollen comforters, Balaclava caps for the Gurkhas and followers, as well as the few British troops that were with the force, and Gilgit boots coming up to the knee, frost-bite and pneumonia would have had most of the force as their victims.

When it got light I went about selecting the thirty ponies from the Tibet Pony Corps. They were a sorry lot—not Tibetan ponies, but the Indian Bazaar pony. They had been very hard worked bringing up rations, and now they were crippled with the unaccustomed cold. The best possible having been selected, bad though they were, and unfit for Mounted Infantry work, they were saddled up and the two bags of grain put on the saddles. As the saddlery had been found too big for mules, it was still worse with these little ponies between twelve and thirteen hands, the girths being in many cases eighteen inches too long. However, there was no help for it then, and they had to be sent off. The Gurkhas had the same trouble with their twenty ponies. They stuck to the pack saddles, and put their two bags of grain on them in the usual manner, laying their Mounted Infantry saddles on top of all. It was a big weight for such small ponies, and the result of the two experiments was practically the same, with the exception that three of the Gurkha ponies did not arrive at Chumbi.

At 9 A.M. the force moved off on the advance into Chumbi, the first stage of a gradual progress which ultimately brought us to Lhasa.

Midwinter is not in itself the most suitable or most agreeable season for entering these desolate and storm-swept highlands. But other considera-

Photo by A. LEWIS & SON.

COLONEL SIR FRANK YOUNGHUSBAND, K.C.I.E., I.A.
British Commissioner in Tibet.

tions were paramount. Colonel Younghusband had spent five fruitless months at Khamba Jong, in Tibetan territory north of Sikkim and Darjeeling, endeavouring to open serious negotiations with properly accredited representatives of Tibet so as to end the long outstanding differences between the two Governments. Boycotted by the Lhasa delegates while the Tibetans proceeded to arm, and unable to retire unsatisfied without loss of national prestige, the Mission had been recalled, only to re-enter Tibet immediately at a more convenient point with the armed support of General Macdonald, who was authorised to advance in the first place as far as Gyantse, more than half-way to Lhasa, and within reach of the capital, should the negotiators still shuffle out of the completion of an agreement.

Over the lofty pass of the Jelap Là (14,350 feet) immediately facing us at Gnatong, lay the Chumbi Valley, 4,000 feet below the summit we were to traverse. This valley, offering at Chumbi itself a convenient winter station for the force, continues northward in its turn, leading higher and higher up the course of the Amu Chu, beyond the level of trees and firewood, to Phari Jong, with its plain, and thence to a second and more gradual pass, the Tang Là, at the foot of the majestic Chumulari. Beyond the Tang Là, again, extends a long mountainous plateau for some seventy miles from Tuna, the first village over the pass, to Gyantse itself; and at Tuna the Mission was prepared to spend the winter as it had spent the summer at Khamba Jong, maintaining itself unmoved on indisputably Tibetan soil until a satisfactory answer should be obtained from Lhasa.

CHAPTER II

THE ADVANCE INTO CHUMBI

ROUGHLY, this was the force that marched off: General Macdonald and Staff; one section, two guns No. 7 British Mountain Battery; two guns, seven-pounders, 8th Gurkhas, carried by coolies, commonly known as Bubble and Squeak; Maxim guns 1st Norfolk Regiment; six companies 23rd Pioneers and two Maxims; four companies 8th Gurkhas; post and telegraph offices. All the baggage had to be carried by a portion of a mule corps that had been working since May in the Teesta Valley, and the Tibet and Cashmire Pony Corps, which had not long been got together. The drivers of the latter were new to their work, and the ponies unused to the height and cold. There was no other transport to be had then, and the Jelap Là had to be surmounted. Extremes did meet certainly, in the worst road, the worst transport, and the greatest altitude that a British army had been asked to work at. Yet all difficulties were cheerfully met and ably overcome. The ground was white with snow when the force started, and, the road being execrable at the best of times, the transport animals soon began to come to grief, and fatigue parties had to be sent out to help them over the first stream that was to be crossed, 500 yards from Gnatong Post. Somebody said it reminded him more of the retreat from Moscow than the advance of a British army.

At 1 P.M. the last of the column was out of sight, and there were left behind at Gnatong five very disappointed officers. The column marched that day as far as Kuppoop, at the foot of the Jelap Là. On the 12th they braced themselves up to a supreme effort, and, getting over the Jelap, arrived at Langram, about 2,000 feet down the other side. This was a terrible descent, as steep as the side of a house, covered with snow, with the ground frozen underneath, so that when the first few troops had passed the path became a regular slide, as slippery as glass, and when the poor ponies and mules came along they had a bad time of it. If an animal fell, it shot down sometimes twenty yards before it could regain its feet.

I believe there was not a single load that was not thrown at least once. The rear-guard did not get into Langram till long after dark, and still quantities of stores and kits were left behind, lost in the dark. Langram is in the pine forest; all, therefore, were able to have a good fire that night, which must have been a consolation after spending a very cold, miserable night at Kuppoop, for, that place being above the wood line, the force had to be satisfied with what fuel could be carried for them—little indeed, but still far better than none.

Early on the morning of the 12th orders were received that one of my companies, under the double-company officer, should proceed that day to Langram in one march. There was just enough transport for them, so they were packed off at once.

I now thought that my luck was dead out, and, feeling that I should stay at Gnatong for the rest of my life, prepared to make the best of it.

On the 13th the force passed through the gate of the Chinese wall at Yatung without opposition. On the contrary, the inhabitants seemed to be very glad to receive and to see the British force. They were tired of Tibetan government and cruelties, and saw in the British force their relief and the prospect of prosperous trade, testifying thereto by immediately bringing in all kinds of supplies for the force. For these they were well paid, to their great astonishment, because they were accustomed to get nothing in return from the Tibetan and Chinese officials when they travelled.

On the 15th the force camped near Chumbi, and were everywhere met with smiling faces by the robust and cheerful people of the country. At Yatung the General and several officers visited Miss Annie Taylor, the missionary lady who has devoted her life to the conversion of the Tibetans and to their civilisation. Her name is, of course, familiar to those who have read her book of travel in Tibet, a book well worth reading by everyone.

The 14th was a very dull day in foggy Gnatong, and in the afternoon Major Beynon, D.S.O., who was commanding, and I went for a walk up one of the mountain ridges with the hope of getting a view of something of Tibet and Butan. Even in this we failed, it being impossible to get far enough and back before dark; but we were well rewarded for our stiff climb through the rhododendron jungle, which is always found on these mountains above the pine forest. Above this nothing in the way of trees or shrubs will grow.

When we left Gnatong it was quite clear, but when we climbed to 1,500 feet above it a thick fog rolled up from the valleys, enveloping and obscuring everything to within 100 feet beneath us. We were just above this mass of fog and cloud, and were still in the sunshine. It was a most wonderful sight. What we saw resembled a great bay of the sea running into the land, on one edge of which we were standing, while the other edge was marked by Kinchenjunga (nearly 28,000 feet high) and all the great snow-peaks round the north of Sikkim, magnificent in their solitary majestic grandeur. We got back to Gnatong about 7 P.M., dined together, and, after airing our several grievances at being left behind, started making plans for the future. A happy idea struck Major Beynon: we would skate. There was an old pond at Gnatong which had been dammed up and used for skating by the British troops stationed there after the '88 campaign. The dam was broken down, and the pond more or less of a mud-puddle. We agreed that it would be excellent exercise for the Pioneers next morning to set to work and build up this dam, so that by the evening we should have a fine piece of ice to skate on, or at least to slide on, as the skates had not yet been ordered.

Hardly had this been decided on when Major Beynon was handed a telegram, which directed that I was to proceed to Chumbi with all expedition to take command of the Pioneer and Gurkha Mounted Infantry, and was to bring along with me as far as Langram so many of my remaining company as transport could be provided for.

At last I had got my orders, and was to see Tibet, and I thanked fortune I was no longer to stagnate at Gnatong. I went to the men and told them I would take half a company into Tibet next day, starting at 6 A.M. They were as pleased as I was, and although it was 10 o'clock at night they got up and began packing there and then.

We marched at 6 A.M. on the 15th, and reached the top of the Jelap Là by noon. A wonderful view of Tibet, Butan, Sikkim, and Nepaul is obtainable from here. Chumulari (nearly 24,000 feet high), in its spotless robe of snow, although sixty miles away, shone in the sun like burnished gold.

Although two companies of the 23rd Pioneers had been working on the road down the pass for two days, it was still an execrable track, frozen hard, down which the mules went sailing gaily. Baggage and all sorts of things lost by the column on the 12th were still lying about, with dead mules and dead ponies in every direction. Several mules and ponies were found grazing, and driven in to Langram. A few days afterwards everything was recovered and handed over to its proper owner. We reached Langram about 3 P.M., where I dropped my half-company, glad indeed that they had to go no further. I went on with eight men, my servant, and six baggage animals. The road led down through the pine-forest, which looked very beautiful as long as the light lasted. The road, however, seemed to be getting worse and worse. It was pitch dark when we passed through Yatung, and the cold was terrible. From Yatung to Richengong is probably not five miles, but it took us five solid hours to get over. In many places the road had stone steps cut or built in it, and these, after the manner of all Tibetan roads, were in a bad state of repair. It was also cut across

FIRST VIEW OF TIBET FROM THE JELAP LA.

by numbers of streams of melted snow, which washed away the soil and left great boulders, so that the passer-by had to skip from one to the other. Now, this is all very well by daytime, and when you know the road, but on a pitch-dark night, when the road is unknown, it is a most unpleasant performance. Down this avenue we tripped, and stumbled, and fell and knocked our shins against the rocks, helping up the baggage animals and replacing the loads which came off every fifty yards.

I have never seen men work better or more cheerfully in very trying circumstances than the eight men with me. Of course Tibet, and for my part the whole of the East, was abused roundly every now and then. Thus we pushed along until we came to a part of the road which had no turning, or at least the road came abruptly to an end, and there was a drop of some fifty feet on the right-hand side, with a roaring torrent at the bottom. We found on getting accustomed to the light that the baggage animals had come to a stop on a sloping edge about three feet wide and could not turn round or go forward or back. The path was a zigzag, and we had missed the turn ; the penalty was the loss of one pony with my tent and mess-box.

It was with the greatest difficulty we succeeded in turning each of the baggage animals round in succession, commencing from the rear; all were got away safely except the one furthest in front. He grew restive, being lonely at his comrades' departure, and, losing his footing, over he went, with all my goods and chattels, including my bedding. To hear that mess-box, which contained all my luxuries, going crash, crash down from rock to rock, was truly heartrending, and I so hungry too!

There was no help for it, so we thanked our stars that we had not gone the way of the mess-box, and pushed ahead. In about another hour we came to a village, which appeared to us in the dark to be as big as a city; this was Richengong. It was 11.40 P.M., and as all the doors were shut, we supposed the inhabitants were either in bed or had taken flight. It really did not matter either, because if they had been there we could not have talked to them, not knowing their language.

After poking about in this village for some time and losing ourselves, at last we struck a road which seemed to be the exit, and having followed it for about two hundred yards, were challenged by one of our own sentries, with his well-known 'Halt! Who goes thar?' and 'Halt, and give de count' sign.' I am afraid he was not answered very politely by his brother Sepoys, but it was all right. What joy! We thought we had joined up with the force; but it was not so: this was

TIBETAN HOUSE.

only a post, with one company of my own regiment. The force was about two miles further on. As we were all fairly done up, we decided to halt for the night. On a bitter cold night it is always a good thing to halt near food and blankets, especially when you have none yourself.

Next morning the men volunteered to go out and look for my kit, and they returned about 8 A.M. with the whole of it. The whisky-bottle even had not been broken, and, still more remarkable, the baggage pony was brought in alive and well, with the exception of many and various cuts. The poor beast was found standing in the water wedged between two rocks.

About 9 A.M. we started off and joined up with the force, which was just leaving camp and proceeding to Chumbi, about three miles further on. The force camped at the junction of the Mu Chu and Rido Chu, a place henceforth known as New Chumbi. At that time there was nothing there, but now several nice snug houses have been built.

That evening I took over the Mounted Infantry of the 23rd Pioneers and 8th Gurkhas. They had little in the way of equipment when they started from Gnatong, but now they had less, and a good deal of what they had was broken. The first thing we did was to shorten the girths, cutting off in some cases eighteen inches. The headstalls, when adjusted, were found to be fitting all right, thanks to the big, ugly fiddle-heads the ponies had. There were no nosebags and few jhools (horse-rugs), and these had to be made up out of empty ration-bags. The ground being frozen, it was next to impossible to drive a wooden peg into it to tether the ponies, and iron pegs were too heavy to carry. These also were affected by the frost, and became so brittle that they used to break like glass while being driven into the ground. There was no rope available, so the ponies had to be hobbled or tied to stones, or made fast as best might be. They were most difficult animals to keep tied up, as they were desperate fighters, and were constantly breaking loose and attacking one another.

We thought we should have a day or two in which to make up the things we wanted, but early next morning we were ordered to reconnoitre ten miles up the road. Major Iggulden accompanied this reconnaissance. The road lay along the left bank of the Amu Chu through beautiful pine forest. About three miles up we saw the formidable Chinese wall and gateway at Gubjong completely blocking the narrow gorge. A Chinese colonel and his staff came out to meet us, and were very friendly, as Chinese mostly are. Three miles further on we came on the Lingmathang Plain, about two miles long and half a mile broad, with the Amu Chu flowing down the centre, and bordered all round with pine forest—a lovely spot and an ideal site for a hill station. Having looked at the road onwards from Lingmathang for about three miles we returned to Chumbi without incident.

CHAPTER III

THE ADVANCE TO PHARI JONG

NEXT day, the 18th, General Macdonald with the force commenced the march to Phari Jong, where we were told we might expect a fight. It is thirty-two miles from Chumbi, and stands about the same height as the Jelap Là, without a tree within fifteen miles of it. We camped at Lingmathang, and as I was advance guard with my fifty Mounted Infantry, I had the opportunity of shooting any game we met on the road, and was fortunate in securing ten blood pheasants, very handsome birds, and a brace of duck.

On the 19th we got as far as Dotha, about a mile above the wood line. Here we made our first acquaintance with real Tibetan wind and cold. Everybody who has been at this camp will agree that it was one of the worst we were in. It was about one thousand yards long and three hundred yards broad, with precipitous mountains at each side running up to 19,000 feet, on which large herds of burrhel were seen, but none bagged. The Amu Chu flows down the centre. The only object of

FROZEN WATERFALL AT DOTHA, 80 FEET HIGH.

interest at Dotha is the beautiful frozen waterfall, quite eighty feet high. It does not add to the warmth of the place. I believe this waterfall was more photographed than anything in Tibet.

The road here from Lingmathang surpassed even the descent from the Jelap Là in its then bad condition. The chief cause of this was that the Amu Chu was frozen with ice four or five feet thick. The melted snow-water which came down in the evening, instead of flowing down the stream, was forced by the ice to find a lower level along the road, which was therefore eaten away till nothing was left of it except enormous boulders. The force had to march up through this snow-water the whole day, till very late in the evening, when it also became frozen. This march tried the country-bred ponies in the transport very much, and several had to be destroyed. The rear guard, on which I happened to be, did not get in till 11 o'clock at night.

Off again next day at 9 A.M. Everybody was in a hurry to get away from Dotha for better or for worse; the next place might be better, but we did not think it could be much worse. Four miles more over the same kind of road, and then we crossed the Amu Chu by the Kamparab Bridge on to the Phari Plain, and were therefore introduced to the bare waste and exalted table-land of Tibet. Nevertheless we were glad to be on open ground, suitable for mounted infantry work; so we rode on and on, but no view of the much-talked-of Phari Jong or fort was yet obtainable. About five miles from the Kamparab Bridge the plain takes a great turn to the left, and on coming to that turn we saw Phari Jong. In the rarefied air one can see so distinctly that it looked quite close, although it was a good four miles off. A most formidable obstacle it looked, so massive and with not an inch of cover anywhere about. Our first impression was, 'If this is held it will take a good deal of taking.' The photograph of Phari will illustrate this better than I can describe it.

On coming within range we opened out to a good distance and rode for it, expecting every yard to be fired at. But no! we were again received with open arms and open doors, just as well as, if not better than, Manning, Turner, and Bogle were received about a hundred years before. The Jongpen assured us that all was perfectly quiet, and that there was no idea of resistance. His statement was not given much credence, since we thought it impossible that the Tibetans would be such fools as not to hold this place, which is a veritable fortress. Just as we got to the other side of the jong an interesting-looking gentleman mounted on a very handsome mule and surrounded by about a hundred warriors, dressed in gorgeous garments and armed with all sorts of curious weapons, came

BREAKING UP CAMP AT PHARI JONG.
TWO WOUNDED MEN, MR. CANDLER AND MAJOR WALLACE DUNLOP.

into view. This personage was taken to be at least the Tibetan Commander-in-Chief. Galloping for the party, we surrounded them, and very frightened they looked when they saw what was happening. We were wrong, however, as the imposing rider of the mule was a Chinese official coming to see Colonel Younghusband, the British Commissioner. A report of all that had happened was sent to General Macdonald, and we proceeded to reconnoitre the Tang Là (15,500 feet), which was much further than we expected, being a good eleven miles from Phari. From the Tang Là we could see Tuna and the great Bam Cho lake, and were at the foot of the snow-clad Chumulari (nearly 24,000 feet), which towered above us like a perpendicular wall of snow. The summit of the Tang Là is difficult to find, as it is a very open pass about five miles wide, and is more like a rolling down than what is understood as a pass.

The ponies were very much spent when they arrived at the top of the pass. Mine lay down under me and began to eat grass. They were greatly in want of water also, for all the streams we had passed were frozen solid, and, much as the ponies tried to break the ice with their fore feet, they could not get a drop to drink. Having rested and fed we commenced our return march to Phari. We were very glad to leave the top of the pass, as the wind was blowing icy cold and numbed us to the bone, notwithstanding poshteens and gloves and all the warm clothes we had on. A short way from the top of the pass we saw our first Tibetan gazelle, a buck, and I was fortunate enough to bag him with one of the men's rifles. His horns were 13¾ inches, which is a little above the average; the biggest I got in Tibet afterwards had horns of 14¼ inches, and I did not hear of a bigger one being secured. They are very pretty and graceful animals, as well as being splendid eating.

As the ponies were so tired we had to walk dismounted nearly all the way back. Darkness soon came on, and we had a miserable time of it making our way across large sheets of ice, sometimes a hundred yards broad, slipping and falling and merely guessing at our direction. Repeatedly one heard a Lee-Metford rifle fall with its owner crash upon the ice, but not a single rifle was damaged; they stand a lot of rough usage. We got back to camp about 8.30 P.M., having been going nearly twelve hours, with only one halt of about an hour on the top of the pass. The fact that we had covered thirty-five miles did not prevent the ponies from breaking loose and fighting all night. They were really insatiable for fighting—much better at that than at anything else. The ground was frozen so hard that what pegs there were, both iron and timber, could not be driven into it; so we tied the ponies in rings, and if they had not been

M.I. PONIES BREAKING HOLES IN THE ICE TO DRINK.

such bad-tempered little brutes they would have been safe enough. They spent most of the night careering through the General's camp, and I was hauled over the coals next morning; but it is an ill wind, &c., for in the end I was promised a new set of picketing gear when we got back to Lingmathang.

I think all who spent that night at Phari have agreed that it was the worst night of their lives. We had to go through much worse later on, but this seemed the worst, I suppose, because we were not used to it, and because the Tibetans did not give any cause for interest or excitement. It was also our first night without firewood, and the local substitute, argol, or yaks' dung, was anything but pleasant fuel, first because we did not know how to light it, and next because of its pungent smoke, which blew in every direction at once. Afterwards when it became a scarce commodity we thought it most excellent stuff.

The force halted the next day, December 21, and I went for a short reconnaissance with the Mounted Infantry. Two companies of the 8th Gurkhas were put into the jong, as also ten Mounted Infantry, post and telegraph offices, supply and transport, all under Major Row, of the 8th Gurkhas, who was henceforth known as the Jongpen, or ruler of the jong. Phari Jong, in spite of its imposing appearance, was old and rickety, and the dirt and filth of ages was collected in it, so that Major Row had plenty of work in making it habitable and sanitary.

The garrison being installed, on the following day the remainder of the force set out on their return to the more hospitable Chumbi. Fourteen miles had to be covered in order to get well into the pine forest and so back to firewood again, and no force ever marched quicker in order to reach the fuel which they valued more than rum.

We arrived at Chumbi on the 23rd, and were uncommonly glad to be back again in comparative comfort, and still more to find that Colonel Younghusband and most of the officers of the Mission had arrived, whereby we were assured that there was now no chance of our going back over the Jelap Là, as camp rumour averred.

The 24th was spent in picking up any good ponies we saw with the transport, and weeding out our bad ones, in improving the saddlery and picketing gear, and casting or repairing all that had been broken or damaged in our first venture to Phari. Late in the evening our Christmas cheer arrived from Darjeeling for the Pioneers' mess, of which I was mess president. The Christmas dinner cost me many anxious moments. If it had not arrived I should have had to face a dozen hungry and angry officers, a contingency I shrank from contemplating. It was a great relief to me

1ST M.I. ON PARADE AT PHARI JONG, WITH CHUMULARI IN THE BACKGROUND.

when turkeys, hams, mincemeat, cakes, plum puddings, champagne, and everything turned up safely. Nineteen sat down to dinner on Christmas Day, and the only thing that fell flat was the champagne, which was so cold that nobody could drink it, and we wished we had ordered beer instead.

On the 26th six companies of the 23rd went to camp three miles above Lingmathang to work on the road, the improvement in which was much appreciated on the next advance. From this camp Major Wallace Dunlop shot the first showa, or Tibetan stag—a ten-pointer, and I believe the first to fall to a white man's gun.

The next week was spent very pleasantly in training the Mounted Infantry, and making a short reconnaissance every day, on each of which we picked up a few of the transport ponies that were lost on the Jelap Là and had strayed. Up to this time no opposition had been offered by the Tibetans, and the general opinion was either that they had no military zeal or spirit or that they were terrible fools, else they could have easily destroyed this very small force with a few men by holding any or all of the uniquely strong natural positions that were available all the way from the Jelap Là to Kamparab Bridge, nine miles from Phari. Phari Jong itself, if held with resolution, could not have been taken by the force, as the ten-pounder guns had only shrapnel shells at that time, and the Gurkha seven-pounder guns, as was proved later, were useless against fortifications, unless they were firing from predominating ground whence they could drop their shells on to an object. In fact, they could not shoot up hill or on the level. All officers with the force who had been through the Tirah campaign or other Indian North-West Frontier expeditions, or South Africa, agreed that they had never seen natural positions as strong as those in Tibet. Consequently the question was often asked, Why did the Tibetans allow the advance of a foreign army through these positions unmolested? It is not difficult to find the answer: they were out-manœuvred by General Macdonald's strategy.

Inasmuch as Colonel Younghusband's Mission, escorted by the 32nd Sikh Pioneers, had been at Khamba Jong in North Sikkim since June 1903, as explained at the end of the first chapter, while the 32nd still occupied Chungu and Tongu on the frontier and Gantak in Sikkim, the Tibetans, thinking that this would be the line of advance, collected a force near Khamba Jong to oppose it. This force was still sitting near Khamba Jong, sixty miles away from Phari as the crow flies, when General Macdonald marched over the Jelap Là and up to Phari. It being midwinter and most of the passes being held by us, news to the opposing army

CHUMULARI.

travelled slowly, so that the Tibetans, having a sublime contempt for us, and implicit confidence in their snow-bound mountain frontier, which no hostile army had ever succeeded in penetrating, did not attempt to move to the succour of Phari Jong till it was too late; and although they did eventually leave their camp at Khamba Jong, they had only reached a place twenty-five miles from Phari Jong when they heard that General Macdonald's force had occupied it. They therefore remained where they were and waited for the further advance which culminated in the affair at Guru on March 31. This accounts for the absence of opposition to the force up to Phari Jong.

CHAPTER IV

THE ADVANCE TO TUNA, AND THE INSTALLATION OF COLONEL YOUNGHUSBAND AND THE MISSION AT TUNA

On January 1, 1904, Lieutenant Bailey, who commanded twenty-five Mounted Infantry raised from the 32nd Sikh Pioneers at Khamba Jong, joined me at Chumbi with his men, bringing the strength of the company up to seventy-five, with two British officers. He had come from Tungu over the Nathu Là, the next pass west of the Jelap Là—a very trying march at that time of year, the altitude of the route being nowhere less than 14,500 feet, while Tungu itself is nearly 17,000. One pony died on the march from exhaustion, and the others were very much spent. They had two clear days' rest at Chumbi before the advance on January 4. The Tibetans having made no attempt to negotiate with Colonel Younghusband at Chumbi, nor taken the slightest notice of his arrival there, while even the rulers of Butan were inclined to be haughty, Colonel Younghusband, with supreme disregard for the time of year and all physical difficulties, decided to proceed to Tuna, beyond Phari and the second great pass, the Tang Là, with the hope of meeting the Chinese Amban and Tibetan delegates there. Therefore on January 4 General Macdonald marched from Chumbi for Tuna with the Mission, and reached Phari Jong once more on the 6th.

The force consisted of six companies 23rd Pioneers, four companies 8th Gurkhas, about seventy Madras and Bengal Sappers and Miners, one section No. 7 British Mountain Battery, Norfolk Maxims, and sixty-five Mounted Infantry in all about one thousand rifles, two guns, and four Maxims. A short march of about six miles to the foot of the Tang Là was done next day. We camped for that night at Chugia, and here for the first time we were told that a night attack by the Tibetans might be expected, notwithstanding the fact that the Mounted Infantry patrols in all directions found no enemy. No attack was made, however, and we arrived at Tuna on the 8th, but as sufficient water was not found at Tuna village, the force camped about three miles beyond, where there was water. Tuna consists of half-a-dozen Tibetan houses of a very poor order. There is not a tree within thirty miles of it. It stands about 15,000 feet above sea-level, on a bare, bleak plain, and in winter or summer is one of the most miserable and uninviting spots on the face of the globe.

The force, although splendidly clad, felt the

cold and the want of firewood very much, and were greatly exhausted by five successive days' marching at those high altitudes. The Mounted Infantry rear guard did not get into camp till 1 A.M., and a few men and coolies did not get in till next day. These were given up as lost, and were expected to have been frozen to death. They had made themselves comfortable for the night by all getting under a tent, without pitching it, but using it as a big blanket, and to everybody's relief turned up in camp next morning just as parties were being sent out to look for them. These Sepoys had done well; they were escorting baggage coolies, who were unable to carry their loads any further, and although they could have easily got into camp themselves, sooner than leave their charge, they remained with the coolies, and were without any food or bedding on a night on which fifty-seven degrees of frost were registered.

Again we were told that a night attack by the Tibetans might be expected, and it was afterwards ascertained that the Tibetans had fully intended to do so, but lost heart at the last moment. They never had a better chance of wiping us out, but they lost it. The cold was so great (fifty-seven degrees of frost) that the bolts of the rifles froze, and the Maxims would not work, in spite of the oil having been carefully wiped off both previously. The men were exhausted, and it was

THE FORCE MARCHING OVER THE TANG LÀ.

very hard to get them to wake up. The sentries were visited every half-hour throughout the night by British and native officers, so these did not get much sleep. The ground was frozen so hard that a shelter trench could not be dug. Everything was in favour of the Tibetans if they attacked, but they did not avail themselves of the opportunity, and never found as good a one again.

Next morning three Mounted Infantry patrols of seventeen men each, under Lieutenant Bailey, Captain O'Connor, R.A., secretary to the Mission (who volunteered), and myself, marched out to look for the enemy. The patrols went in different directions, and returned to camp about 5.30 P.M. with much news, and none empty-handed. Lieutenant Bailey came across four Tibetan mounted soldiers armed to the teeth, but as they bolted off on seeing him, he gave chase and captured all four. One of these proved to be cook to the Tibetan general, who doubtless was very cross when his chef did not return to cook his dinner that night. They were questioned and released next day.

Captain O'Connor found a fine flock of sheep being driven towards the enemy's camp, so he changed their direction and brought them to our camp. These were paid for in hard cash. My own party were going along the foot of the hills that edge the Tuna plain, and were about twelve miles from camp when we heard Tibetan guns being fired to the north of us, whereupon we rode up the hills as fast as we could in the direction of the firing. We thought that one of the other patrols had met and were engaged with the enemy, and we were annoyed at being out of it. The tops of the hills were more or less flat, and we got on faster, till we could see into the next valley; then, as the firing was now very close, we dismounted, and peeped over the brow of the hill into the valley. A sight met our gaze which cheered all our hearts up. There at last was the Tibetan army we had heard so much about, in two camps, between 2,000 and 3,000 of them, about 500 feet below us, and only 1,100 yards off. Although we were only seventeen rifles we could have given them a very unpleasant half-hour of it, but we were still a peaceful Mission, and were not allowed to fire unless attacked, and then in self-defence. This army was about eleven or twelve miles from our camp, and the firing we heard was not an engagement with another patrol, but simply the discharging of old charges from their guns in order to load them up freshly to ensure no misfires.

As we got heliographic communication with our own camp, the General heard all about the Tibetan army ten minutes after we found them, and I was directed to remain in observation, and return to camp by dark. The Tibetans did not find out that we were looking at them for at least three hours after we first saw them, and then, seeing the position we held, and not knowing how many of us were there, they thought discretion the better part of valour, and did not molest us.

On the way back to camp two Tibetans carrying provisions to the Tibetan army were brought in to be questioned, after which they were immediately let go again.

During the day a fortified post was constructed at Tuna, and was occupied by Colonel Younghusband and the Mission, the Norfolk Maxims, four companies of the 23rd, and ten Mounted Infantry, under general command of Colonel Hogge, of the 23rd. All the rations with the force were left with them, and we went back to Phari Jong the next day in one march (twenty miles). The same day, the 9th, the first hostile act on the part of the Tibetans took place at Phari Jong. It will be remembered that two companies of the 8th Gurkhas garrisoned Phari Jong, and the orders in force were that the Tibetan residents in the Jong were not to leave it without the permission of the officer commanding. Two Lamas of rank disregarded these orders, and were leaving the jong followed by a crowd of retainers and hangers-on, when they were met by Lieutenant Grant, of the 8th, and his orderly, the latter carrying a rifle and bayonet. Lieutenant Grant attempted to detain the Lamas, and caught hold of one of their bridles, but was not in any way aggressive to them. The Lama shouted something in Tibetan to his followers, who immediately began throwing large stones. One of these hit Lieutenant Grant on the forehead, knocking him down and fracturing his skull. The orderly was also knocked down and his rifle seized and carried off by the two Lamas, who escaped and went straight for the Tibetan camp we had discovered that day. Lieutenant Grant was very severely injured, and still suffers from the effects of his wounds, although he remained with his regiment and took part in the capture and assault of Gyantse Jong on July 6.

The force halted at Phari Jong from the 11th to the 18th, and during this time a good understanding was come to with the Butanese and the local Tibetans. The yak drivers agreed to hire out and work their yaks for transport purposes, and local supplies such as fodder, tsampa (barley flour), and grain, began to come into Phari, which was to become the further main supply depot.

On the 13th I was sent as escort to a convoy of rations to Tuna with fifty Mounted Infantry and a hundred of the 32nd Pioneers, and camped five miles from Phari that day. Convoy work now was not difficult as we had a splendid mule corps to work with, the 12th, commanded by Captain C. Moore, S. and T. Corps. This corps, as will be seen, was the first to come up from India and the last to go back. The animals worked through

M.I. CARRYING MAILS OVER THE TANG LÀ.

the worst of the winter, and did more marching in Tibet than any other corps, yet they were always fit, in spite of the extra loads we used to try to put on them, which, when discovered, used to draw forth furious wrath from their commander.

The next day five hundred rifles and the section No. 7 Mountain Battery, came out from Phari to see us to the top of the Tang Là, and we were met by two companies of the 23rd Pioneers, who came out from Tuna four miles.

This strong escort was, after all, unnecessary, as the Tibetans did not attempt to attack or even show themselves. It was too cold for even Tibetans to take the initiative.

At 9 o'clock next morning, mounting the 100 men of the 32nd Pioneers and all the mule-drivers on the mules, and wrapping them all up in blankets and rezais, we marched back to Phari Jong, twenty miles, in exactly five hours.

We had found at Tuna that Colonel Younghusband, the Mission, and escort had settled themselves as comfortably as circumstances would permit. They complained most of the unpleasantness of the pungent argol smoke, and the choking, stifling sensation at night when they wanted to sleep, caused by the high altitude, to which they had not yet become accustomed.

On the 18th the whole force, with the exception of the two companies of Gurkhas, left Phari Jong for Chumbi, where they arrived on the 19th to take up their winter quarters, all glad to be back among wood fires again. I was halted at Lingmathang Plain, as it was considered to be the best place possible for the training of mounted infantry, and we remained there for exactly two months, the pleasantest time I spent in Tibet.

PANORAMA OF LINGMATHANG.

CHAPTER V

THE PREPARATIONS FOR THE ADVANCE TO GYANTSE—AT CHUMBI AND LINGMATHANG

It was with great pleasure I received orders from Major Iggulden, the Chief Staff Officer, that my company was to be raised to one hundred strong, and that I was to go and select ten more men from the 23rd Pioneers and sixteen from the 32nd.

This seemed to be real business, but when I asked for three trained native officers to be brought up from India, I was told I could not have them, and that I must manage as best I could with the one native officer I had (Jemadar Prem Singh, 9th Gurkha Rifles). In a few days I got the extra men, but I had no ponies, and there were none to be bought. Gradually we obtained ponies and also a few Tibetan riding mules, which were splendid animals for mounted infantry work, although they were a good deal more expensive.

The real training of the men and ponies now began. Riding schools were built and lines laid out, and all made up their minds to learn and to work. It was good work, although hard, especially on account of the terrible cold, but the men all felt that they would probably confront an enemy some day, and it was well to prepare for him. Those who were not apt or did not care to work were sent back to their regiments and others came in their place.

The hardest thing of all to get into their heads was that the grooming of their ponies was a necessity, and not meant to be a fatigue. The number of line sentries needed at night came very heavy on the men. These were required to look after the combative ponies, and to tie them up when they broke loose, which was often, as we still had only head-ropes and bits of string until the men made up heel-ropes out of empty ration-bags. Gradually things were got together. Riding-breeches for the men came from the clothing department. These were a great boon to them, as their serge trousers wore out in one march, and the men also were terribly chafed, actually bleeding, from this much-too-loose garment. New canvas nosebags, hoof-picks, head-ropes, brushes, curry-combs and dubbing came to hand, and activity reigned everywhere.

So it was with General Macdonald also—collecting his 20,000 maunds of rations at Phari Jong for the next advance, organising the transport, raising new transport, completing his field park and ammunition column, and making and improving the roads in Sikkim over the Jelap Là and the Nathu Là, and all the way from Chumbi to Phari.

The 32nd Pioneers, now no longer required in the Khamba Jong direction, were brought into Chumbi, as also the remainder of the 8th Gurkhas, so that the force now began to assume decent proportions. I was pleasantly surprised one day by a visit from the Chief Staff Officer, who came to have a general look round and see how the Mounted Infantry venture was getting on, especially when he said that I could have three more native officers from India. These were what I wanted most of all, and I asked for Subadar Sangat Singh, 45th Rattray's Sikhs, Jemadar Hazara Singh, 16th Cavalry, and Jemadar Thakur Singh, 47th Sikhs. They arrived in about a week, and completed the company of four sections, each of which had in it twenty-five rifles, one native officer, and one from amongst the two British officers, the nalbund (shoeing smith), and the Tibetan interpreter, so that each section was twenty-seven strong and had twenty-seven ponies, and the strength of the company was 108.

As the native officers had arrived I could afford time to pay some attention to the showa (or Tibetan stag), ovis ammon, and burrhel, to the beautiful blood pheasants, tragopan, minall, Tibetan partridge, various kinds of duck, teal, and the goosander, all of which could be got within reach of Lingmathang, and many a pleasant day they gave me. To get at the burrhel and ovis ammon in any case entailed a long and stiff climb, as they lived on the top of the snow-capped hills 4,000 to 5,000 feet above the plain; and often, although it would be a clear day when one set out, the hills would be in fog or enveloped in a snow-storm when the summit was reached, so that the climb had been done to no purpose, and on these occasions it was most difficult to find the way down again. One time we did not get back to camp till 2 A.M., having been completely lost in a blizzard. We found that the whole company had gone out in all directions looking for us, and when we did get back, it was quite two hours before the company was collected again.

Until now I did not know what a real good fellow the Sepoy is, and what a regard and anxiety he has for the safety and comfort of his British officers. Whenever I was out of camp after dark, the men of their own accord, without any orders, would start off a piquet of five or six men to meet me; and when, as often happened, I used to go to the General's camp at Chumbi, five miles away, these men would come along the road until they met me, or walk into Chumbi, to find me and act as escort home. I shall always have pleasant recollections of the kind and thoughtful actions

SUBADAR SANGAT SINGH, SIRDAR BAHADUR, MY TIBETAN INTERPRETER AND SHIKARI, WITH A PAIR OF BURRHEL.

the men did for me, Sikhs and Gurkhas alike, both equally good, and real sportsmen.

The showa in his habits is very similar to the Cashmire stag, and at that time of the year—January, February, and March—lies up all day in the densest part of the forest, and only comes out to graze and drink late in the evening, returning very early in the morning. To get a shot at him, therefore, one had to climb up the hill about 4 P.M. or 3 A.M. and sit waiting over a bit of running water that had escaped being frozen, or some open space where he was likely to come out and graze. Being very keen to shoot a stag, I took every opportunity I could, but never even saw a doe for over a month. The cold was terrible, always about thirty-five degrees of frost, but the desire was greater. At length, one morning in the beginning of March a Gurkha and I were toiling up a hill when the Gurkha pointed out to me seven showa far above us. It was just dawn, and not light enough to distinguish which was the stag. We waited till we could make out the stag, and then my Lee-Metford bullet passed clean through his body, but being a big, strong animal, standing about 14.3, he went off, although showing signs of being badly hit. We tracked him for about a mile, and expected to get him any moment, as he had lain down several times, and was evidently becoming weaker. But then occurred the most unfortunate thing that could happen to us, a storm of snow; down it came, driven along by a fierce wind, completely obliterating the stag's track, as well as numbing us to the bone. It was useless going any further, so we had to give him up, and returned to camp very much down in our luck.

On February 8 we joined General Macdonald's column, escorting a big convoy with stores for Tuna, which we reached on the 11th. There we found Colonel Younghusband as cheerful as ever notwithstanding the miserable existence he and the other officers with him were leading.

Pneumonia had claimed several men of the 23rd and a number of the followers, while nearly everybody had a severe cough. The men who seemed to have stood the severe cold and privations best of all were those of the 1st Norfolk Machine Gun Detachment; nothing ever disturbed these men, be it cold, or short rations, or bullets.

We arrived back at Lingmathang on the 14th without mishap. There were many cases of frost-bite amongst the mule-drivers and men of the escort, which I am thankful to say we escaped. This opportunity was taken to change the Mounted Infantry men and ponies at Tuna and Phari Jong.

About a fortnight later we had to escort another convoy to Tuna again, and as the wind and cold were as bad as ever, we began to think that we should never have a comfortable day in Tibet.

M.I. MAKING ROAD OVER THE TANG LA.

During this visit to Tuna we heard some interesting news of the Tibetans. They had shifted their headquarters from the camp in which they were originally found on January 9, to the Hot Springs at Guru, the leaders making themselves comfortable in the village of Guru, on the Lhasa road, about eleven miles from Tuna. Colonel Younghusband used to receive and send letters to them, and invited their General and chief Lamas to visit him at Tuna, with a small escort of their personal servants. They did come, but they brought an armed following of about 1,000 men with them. These of course were told that they could not be permitted to come nearer than a mile to the Tuna Camp. This interview was fruitless, as the Tibetan officials had no power delegated to them by the Lhasa authorities to treat with Colonel Younghusband, and all they could say was that he must go back to Yatung (the nominal trading station immediately north of the Jelap Là), where they would discuss their differences with the British Commissioner. Colonel Younghusband replied that it was getting on for a year since he went to Khamba Jong, and there waited patiently for their representatives to meet him, but they had not done so, nor condescended even to answer his letters. Eventually they left Tuna in just as obstinate a frame of mind as when they arrived.

The Tinpuk Jongpen of Butan visited Colonel

Younghusband at Tuna, and was received with befitting ceremony. He advised the Tibetans also to come to terms with the British, as it was useless opposing them. To him also they turned a deaf ear. A few days later Colonel Younghusband conceived and carried out a most daring act. He rode straight into the Tibetan camp without an escort of any kind, and only accompanied by two British officers and an interpreter. He gave the Tibetans no notice of his visit, and so surprised them that they had not time to make up their minds to take his life or make him a prisoner. In the conversation that ensued the Tibetans got very excited and vociferous in their demands to 'go back to Yatung,' and Colonel Younghusband had to use all his *savoir faire* and tact to soothe them down again and prevent them from committing any further indiscretion. His impression was that the General was inclined to be reasonable, but that the head Lama, who had equal power with the General, was the stumbling-block.

By this visit Colonel Younghusband wished to impress on the Tibetans that he trusted them, that he was not afraid of them, and that he was making every effort to treat with them amicably, and not by force. But it was all lost on the Tibetans, who were much too obstinate, proud, and haughty, and held us too much in contempt to listen to reason.

They also relied on their old strategy which they so successfully applied against both the Sikhs under Zarawar Singh, in 1840–41—the destruction of whose army compelled the Maharajah of Cashmire to pay triennial tribute to the Dalai Lama—and the Gurkhas at Shigatse over a hundred years ago, where the Gurkha army was treacherously cut to pieces. The Tibetans thought that they would allow us also to get well into the heart of their country, and when we were far from our base, and beyond the reach of succour, they would surround us and cut us up—tactics which they tried to apply at Gyantse, in the following May and June.

After we got back to Lingmathang, heavy snow fell every day, and there was much difficulty in getting grass for the ponies, as it was all snowed up, and the people could not cut it. It was so heavy that the burrhel had to leave their hill-tops and come down close to the plain to pick up any grass that showed above the ground. The two best heads I got were 25½ inches and 24 inches. Even the showa paid visits to the plain, and on the morning of March 17 a showa doe gave us splendid sport and capital practice in riding for the Mounted Infantry. The company were out exercising on the plain, all riding bare-back and each man leading one or two other ponies, when I was told a female showa had appeared. I sprang on the first pony I could catch, and told all the men to give chase, which they did with great spirit. Many came to grief; but it did not matter—no sooner had they fallen off than they were up again. There was a small stream crossed by a plank bridge about three feet wide; two men went for this bridge at full gallop, and colliding, both they and their ponies fell off the bridge into the water through the thin ice. Many other most amusing incidents occurred, but after about forty minutes of a real good run up and down the plain, I got my pony level with the showa, and had the good luck to get my arm round her neck. This unaccustomed weight on her brought her to the ground, and we rolled down the slope till we ended up in a big rose-bush. Here Subadar Sangat Singh came to my assistance, and got hold of her hind leg, and a tough job he had to retain his grip. The Sepoys followed up quickly, and she was secured and led off to camp. At the shoulder she stood quite 14.3. On the 19th I had to leave Lingmathang, and the people told off to look after her gave her salt, from which she died. Had she lived she would have been presented by the company to his Majesty the King, as this animal was the first of its kind ever caught.

MEN OF THE 1ST M.I. BRINGING THE SHOWA INTO CAMP.

CHAPTER VI

THE ADVANCE TO GYANTSE AND THE GURU AND ZAMTUNG GORGE FIGHTS

St. Patrick's Day, March 17, 1904, was a record day for the Mounted Infantry, for, besides the sport they had in capturing the showa, and a dram of rum per man which I gave them in honour of my birthday and the Patron Saint, we got our orders to leave Lingmathang for good, and proceed once more to Phari Jong, where we were to be actively employed—in what way we did not know, but the simple fact was enough to arouse intense excitement. Our place at Lingmathang was taken by the 2nd (or Pathan) Mounted Infantry, commanded by Captain Peterson, of the 46th Punjabis. This company was mounted on very good country-bred ponies, and well equipped at Siliguri. Its advent caused much sorrow amongst my men, who thought that their little ponies would never be able to live with these fine country-breds, and that they would be left on the lines of communication. It was extraordinary the number of men who brought up their ponies to be cast, saying one would not eat his food, another had a sore back, or was gone in the legs, or too weak or blind; one man even declared that his pony was too ugly to ride. They were only pacified by being told that they could have new ponies when they captured them from the enemy in a fight. This pleased them very much, and doubtless they all registered vows that this should be done; in any case they did capture ponies later on. Great was their joy, therefore, when we were told to leave Lingmathang the day before the 2nd Mounted Infantry arrived.

That evening I was ordered down to headquarters at Chumbi to be told by the General what he wished us to do at Phari. The General Officer Commanding had decided to advance to Gyantse at once to forestall the enemy, but he had not sufficient transport, and knew that the few hired yaks and Tibetan drivers would not work beyond Phari Jong for fear of their own people. He therefore wanted as many yaks as were within a day's march from Phari to be rounded up, with their saddles and drivers, and brought into Phari. This had to be done in one day, else those not brought in would have gone off to the Tibetan camp at Guru. The General needed at least 700, saying that it was a very serious matter for the force, and that it was our job to catch them. Well, nothing could be better for us; we were to be

THE COLDEST SPOT IN ASIA. STRIKING CAMP AT DOTHA.

tried at last, and we were to act by ourselves and on our own resources. We had no idea of the whereabouts of the yaks, but they had to be got. The one limitation laid on us was that we were not to interfere with the Tibetans in their camp at Guru beyond the Tang Là.

On the 18th we left Lingmathang, not without regrets, as our time there had been very pleasant, and we knew there were many more uncongenial and inhospitable places in Tibet. Of this we were thoroughly convinced on our arrival at our camp, Dotha, which was known as the coldest place in Asia, and was never more worthy of its name than on this particular evening. The frozen waterfall was bigger than ever. There was a hurricane blowing down the defile, accompanied by a heavy fall of snow. Tents were useless, as they were blown down almost as soon as they were put up, and those that did remain standing were quickly filled by the driven snow. The men could not cook any food, nor the ponies or mules eat any fodder. It was so bad that the Mussulman mule-drivers asked for rum, which they are so strictly prohibited from drinking by their religion. About three feet of snow fell that night, and our start from camp next day was most difficult and trying, and we were all pleased to get that afternoon to Phari, where the snow had not lain. The evening was spent in finding out all that was known of yaks from Captain Tillard, who from his experience of the Nepal yaks was a great authority on that animal and all connected with it.

At dawn the following day the company started on its yak drive. The native officers and myself, with about twenty men each, issued from Phari Jong in different directions and went straight ahead till we found yaks, which were immediately sent in. The last native officer with his drove turned up at midnight. There were all kinds of yaks, splendid beasts, many over sixteen hands, great, powerful, shaggy fellows. Then there were cows, and some too young to work; in all, the company had collected 1,720, out of which Captain Tillard selected 750. The others were let go again. The Sepoys looked on in silent satisfaction while the yaks were being counted over, and each considered himself thoroughly rewarded for a hard day's work on receipt of General Macdonald's kind and courteous telegram of approval. Now we had to turn our thoughts to mules and ponies, numbers of which were known to be about, but nothing would induce the Tibetans to bring them in and sell them, as they were so afraid of the tortures that would most certainly be inflicted on them by the Lhasa authorities for helping the British, in whose power to protect them they disbelieved. As no ponies or mules had been seen for a long time, the officers at Phari had come to

1ST M.I. CAMP AND CAPTURED YAKS AT PHARI JONG, WITH TELEGRAPH WIRE IN FOREGROUND.

the conclusion that there were none. However, a thorough investigation of Phari village and the underground cellars proved the contrary. The Mounted Infantry, dismounted this time, were split up into parties, the commanders of which were pointed out the parts of the village that they had to search, by signal from the top of the jong, whence a good view was obtained. This expedition resulted in the unearthing of 131 good mules and ponies, which caused the men still more satisfaction, as they had already selected their mounts.

The Tibetans did not make any resistance, and in their hearts they were uncommonly glad that their village was being raided, as they had seen the large prices paid to the yak drivers for their yaks, and knew that they would also receive anything they asked for their animals, so they all turned up smiling to be paid. They had saved their faces also with regard to their own countrymen, and they had no reluctance in asking three times the value of a mule or pony. Fifteen thousand maunds of rations (a maund is eighty pounds) had been stored at Phari ; transport was available, and General Macdonald with the force left Chumbi on the 23rd, arriving in Phari on the 26th, where they halted for one day, and on the 28th marched for Tuna, which was reached on the 29th. We crossed the Tang Là in a freezing snowstorm so thick that one could not see twenty yards in front.

It was too cold to ride, so we plodded along on foot. On reaching the top the men presented the funniest spectacle that could be imagined. They looked like pictures of Father Christmas, especially the Sikhs, as their beards, hair, eyebrows, and eyelashes were encrusted in frozen snow, with icicles hanging down, reminding one of walruses, and bright red faces that had been skinned by the cutting wind.

At Tuna we found Colonel Younghusband, the Mission, Colonel Hogge, and the escort in great spirits, being thankful that their weary and uninteresting watch of nearly three months was over. During this time they had been subject to greater cold and discomfort than any British force had ever encountered before, and well they all stood it. Never a word of discontent was heard from the British Tommy of the Norfolk Regiment, or the Sepoys or the followers. The death-rate from pneumonia amongst the native ranks had been heavy, but did not disturb the remainder in their duty.

The Tibetan army were still sitting at Guru, and owing to our long delay in advancing, complacently imagined that they had frightened us into not making a further advance.

The force halted on the 30th, and all spare transport was sent back to Phari to bring up more supplies. I was sent out with half the company to reconnoitre as much of the hills as possible, and to find out if there was more than one Tibetan army in the vicinity. We kept going for sixteen hours, and had only one halt for twenty minutes to feed; in that time we covered quite sixty miles, and had been up to 17,000 feet. Late in the evening we were riding down a spur towards home from which we could see the village of Guru and the Tibetan camp about two miles away, when we noticed that we were passing through a sangared position. The sangars (or stone fortifications) were very massive and well loopholed. This was where the Tibetans meant to oppose us; it was unoccupied now, and there was not a man to be seen even in the camp or village. It was too cold for even a Tibetan soldier to be out. Tuna and our camp were still eleven miles away, and as it was getting dark we made the best of our way back. The reconnaissance was useful so far as information was concerned, but afforded no excitement, nor encounter with the enemy. At 8.15 A.M. on March 31 the force fell in at Tuna in six inches of snow, and marched to the Tibetan position at the Hot Springs near the village of Guru. It consisted of about 1,000 rifles, two guns of No. 7 Mountain Battery, two Maxims Norfolk Regiment, Bubble and Squeak, as the two Gurkha guns have been known for years, and the 1st and 2nd Mounted Infantry.

The Hot Springs flow out of the base of a spur at the western end of the Bam Cho Lake, and the village of Guru is about three miles further on at the foot of the next spur. At one time the lake washed the foot of the hills, but has receded, and is now quite two miles distant. The Lhasa authorities were ignorant of this fact, and believing that the lake was still close up to the hills, ordered their army to hold what they thought was a narrow gorge, instead of being an open plain, which could be marched round from any direction. About four miles from Tuna a Tibetan courier rode up to Colonel Younghusband and gave him a peremptory order to halt, and to advance no further, otherwise there would be trouble. Colonel Younghusband replied that as the Tibetan officials would not come to him, he must go to them. A few miles further on two more couriers rode up to say that the force must halt and wait till the Tibetan officials could find it convenient to come out. They were told that it was unnecessary to halt so far away, and give the Tibetan officials the trouble of coming such a distance. About two miles from the Hot Springs, the Tibetan General and the Lhasa Lama, with a quantity of smaller fry and an escort of about thirty men, all armed with some kind of small-bore rifle, or revolver, met Colonel Younghusband. The force was immediately halted, and Colonel Younghusband, the

CHUMULARI AND SIXTY MILES OF MOUNTAINS REFLECTED IN THE BAM CHO LAKE.

General, and their respective Staffs, escorted by about twenty men, moved on about 800 yards ahead of the force, to meet the Tibetans. All dismounted and sat on the ground to discuss matters. The Tibetans were insulting and truculent, and reiterated their demand that we should go back to Yatung on pain of meeting with sore trouble. They were told that the Mission must go on to Gyantse, and were asked to take their men off the road, to prevent any chance of a contretemps. Colonel Younghusband used every effort to bring them to reason, but they obstinately refused to give way an inch. They were then told that we would proceed, and they returned to their sangars and wall at the Hot Springs. As we approached we saw that all the sangars, which had been empty the evening before, were now packed with armed Tibetans, the wall across the road was manned, and the rocks and crags above swarmed with the enemy.

We were doing right flank guard and would pass about 800 yards from these rocks; inside us were two companies of the 23rd Pioneers. On we went, getting closer and closer and wondering when the Tibetans would fire the first shot and take advantage of the splendid opportunity we gave them. (We were not meant to attack them, and were ordered not to fire on any account.) When level with the Hot Springs we were all halted. Two more companies of the 23rd went straight up to the wall and the Gurkhas and 2nd Mounted Infantry, doing left flank guard, went up the hill to the sangars. The Tibetans were then told that they must either clear out or lay down their arms. They would not do either, whereupon the Sepoys were told to take their arms away from them. This went on very quietly for a time. There was a solitary rock about 600 yards in rear of the wall, behind which about 100 Tibetans were collected. I was directed to go with one section of Mounted Infantry and turn them out, after taking away their arms. We went up to them and told them what they had to do; after a little demur they obeyed, and left with us a very fine jingal, the first we had seen. This fired a leaden bullet two pounds in weight and carried up to 2,500 yards.

We were standing in the open on the road, talking to the Tibetans, when from the direction of the wall we heard a single shot, which was not a Lee-Metford. A few minutes afterwards our Lee-Metfords rattled out, and as we were straight in the line of fire, their bullets came right amongst us. It can be imagined with what agility we got under the shelter of that solitary rock; but the Tibetans also thought it was a good place to make for, and tried to drive us out, whereupon arose what is called in Ireland 'an argument,' of which they got the worst.

SCENE OF THE FIGHT AT GURU.

But we had no luck, because when the gunners opened fire, the first thing that caught their eye was this rock and the Tibetans surrounding it: they had not noticed that a small party of us were behind it also, so they loosed off at and over the rock, which made us all the fonder of it.

Now, this outburst of shooting came about as follows. Nobody in the British force, at the phase which the disarming of the Tibetans had reached, expected it or wished it to take place, but it became necessary in self-defence.

The disarming was going on at the wall perfectly quietly when a Tibetan fired a pistol at a Sikh, and wounded him very severely in the face. Other Tibetan swordsmen drew their swords, and rushed at Major Dunlop, of the 23rd Pioneers, and Mr. Candler, the correspondent of the 'Daily Mail,' who was sitting on the ground almost in the midst of the Tibetans, writing a telegram to his paper to the effect that the Tibetans had given in without a shot being fired. These two were terribly slashed about. Mr. Candler was saved by his poshteen, on which he had seventeen cuts. His left hand was almost severed above the wrist, and had to be amputated, and his right hand was cut across the back so badly that for some time little hope of saving it was entertained. Major Dunlop lost the first and second fingers of his left hand. There were certainly 1,500 Tibetans at the wall, and had they not been fired on promptly they would have rushed on and easily cut up the 150 Sepoys confronting them.

On the outbreak of the firing the Tibetans in the sangars on the hill began throwing stones and firing on the Gurkhas and 2nd Mounted Infantry, and then the fight became general. The Tibetans retreated to the Guru village, and were followed by the force, the two companies of Mounted Infantry leading. Guru village was rushed and cleared, and then they retreated along the Gyantse road, on which we followed them for twelve miles and thoroughly dispersed them. Knowing that the General was hard up for transport, while I was in want of ponies, my main object was to capture all their animals, and we succeeded in getting 131 yaks and sixteen ponies and mules. Camp at Tuna was reached about 9 P.M., and glad we were to get there, bad as it was. A piercing wind was blowing in the faces of the force on the march back, which was so strong that it considerably hindered the infantry and followers in marching.

Behind the solitary rock we had one native officer and two men wounded, two ponies killed and two wounded. In the pursuit another man was slightly wounded by a sword-cut.

The owners of the two ponies that were killed gave us cause for a good laugh, as they were very angry that the Tibetans presumed to do the Sirkar (British Government) so much harm as to kill two ponies; they did not express any sympathy for their wounded comrades, and only thought of the loss and what they should do without their mounts. They were very much relieved when I told them they had better catch some of the Tibetan ponies that were wandering about, and the next day they showed me two very good animals that they had secured.

After the fight Guru village was held by two companies of the 32nd Pioneers and the 2nd Mounted Infantry.

The force halted at Tuna till April 4, when the march to Gyantse commenced. On April 2 we reconnoitred Phram, on the other side of Bam Cho Lake, and found that the Tibetans had fortified a position there also to block that road to Gyantse, and that it had been occupied by about 2,000 men. When they heard the result of the Guru fight, they beat a hasty retreat to Kangma, where they built a wall about a mile long, and then to the Zamtung Gorge, where they fought.

Enough stores and transport had been brought to Tuna by the evening of the 3rd, and the General ordered the march for Gyantse to commence on the 4th.

We marched off full of hopes and with light hearts. There was no drawing back now, and it was felt that a campaign was really being begun. The transport, or menagerie as it was called, was in good order, and consisted of mules, ponies, bullocks, ekkas (Indian carts), yaks, coolies, and donkeys (the Royal Donkey Corps, raised by Captain Pollock Morris, Royal Highlanders); they all came trooping along like the animals out of the Ark.

Mounted Infantry work was now in full swing, and the two companies did advanced flank and rear guards on alternate days, reconnoitring up to ten miles in front of the force every day, each company doing about thirty-four miles every other day, besides bringing the post up from the rear.

On the 6th Kalatso was reached, and the second big lake was passed. The 2nd Mounted Infantry during their reconnaissance ahead struck the enemy again holding the village of Tsemundoo. The orders were that the Tibetans were not to be fired on unless they fired on us first, and in carrying out this order Captain Peterson and Lieutenant Bailey, of the 2nd Mounted Infantry (the latter had been transferred temporarily), and Captain Cowie, R.E., nearly lost their lives through treachery on the part of the Tibetans. Captain Peterson had halted his company about 800 yards from the village, and the three officers, having dismounted, walked up alone to talking distance from the village and asked that a Tibetan should be sent out to confer with them. This the Tibetans agreed to, and said that their spokesman was coming. Immediately upon this the officers, thinking them to be friendly, went a little closer, when a volley of about 200 Tibetan guns and rifles was fired at them. They had a miraculous escape, the bullets having all gone high, and wounded one of the ponies far behind.

As the enemy were occupying a fortified village and evidently in large numbers (about 500), and the officers were alone, there was nothing left for them to do but to go off *ventre à terre*. The Pathan Mounted Infantry had not trusted the enemy, and a few of them had covered with their rifles five or six Tibetans, whom they saw sitting behind a wall in the village, and as soon as the Tibetan fire commenced, crack went their rifles, and silenced the hostile party.

It was our turn to go ahead next day, but the enemy had thought better of it and evacuated Tsemundoo that morning, and retreated to Kangma. We captured a few of their transport animals, but did not come up with the men, as they had gone too far; we heard, however, from Tibetans we met that they had stopped at Kangma.

The following morning Captain Peterson was *en avant*, and about 3.30 P.M. sent a message to the General that he had again located the Tibetans near Kangma, that they had built a wall right across the valley and up the hills on the right, and that a few shots had been exchanged. It was too late to attack them that day. Next day at 9 A.M. the General started off in fighting array, intending to drive them from their position. But vigorous treatment was not required, as they had departed during the night, abandoning another fine position to us. We were advanced guard that day, and late in the evening came up with them again at the Zamtung Gorge, which we had heard so much about as being a very narrow and difficult defile, and so it is. On coming to the gorge, the road and valley seem blocked in front by a spur extending towards the right about 1,500 feet high. The road along the bottom of the defile bears to the right also for about a mile. Here the valley widens out to about 150 yards, with a length of some 800 yards. On the left the cliffs are perpendicular, solid walls of rock, on the right the rocky slopes could be climbed by infantry with great difficulty—a regular scramble. The heights to the right are about 2,000 feet. In front, at first sight, there seems to be no outlet: the road and valley seem to end up in the side of a steep rocky hill covered with huge boulders, and the stream seems to disappear into some subterranean cavern. What happens is this: The defile, road, and stream take a sharp turn to the left round the foot of the precipitous spur, and this cannot be seen till one arrives actually at the corner. The defile then opens out, the stream still hugging the left. It was at this corner the Tibetans hoped to stop us, and they were quite right in their choice of position, as they had a good line of retreat, and the strongest of positions to hold. The road round the corner through the boulders was only six feet wide for about 500 yards.

In the reconnaissance on the evening of the 9th we had just got into the defile when we were fired at by Tibetan jingals from sangars on the spur to the left. For some time we could not make out the position of the jingals, as their bullets were falling too high above us on our right, and they were too far away for us to see their smoke quickly. A few of their transport animals were seen going down the defile with unbecoming haste; these were captured, and then we retired to a more respectful distance and halted under the cover of some ruined walls, taking a good look at their position, and sketching as much as could be seen of it then. We saw the first tree we had set eyes on for nine days, and this news caused nearly as much excitement in camp as the fact that the Tibetans were holding a very strong position in front.

The distribution of the company now was as follows: Five men, including three signallers, permanent escort to General Officer Commanding; five at Tuna; five at Guru; one native officer and seventeen men at Kangma; ten Gurkhas escort to the Ekka Corps; one native officer and nine men (Gurkhas) escort to the Yak Corps, leaving two native officers and fifty-one men with me. The men wounded at Guru all came along and were left with the baggage daily. They would not stay behind on any account.

The following morning, April 10, the General determined to force the defile. I was sent on ahead to have another look at the enemy, and see if they were still there or had bolted. Very glad we were when they again saluted us with a jingal volley. We waited till the General and force came up. Then the Gurkhas were sent up the hill on the left to take the enemy on their right flank and drive them off the high spur running towards our right front. It was calculated that it would take three hours for the Gurkhas to get into position, as the shaly slopes were very steep and exceedingly difficult going. The seven-pounder guns went up the hill on the right to support the Gurkhas when they were ready to attack, and the rest of us sat down and waited. One of my sections was put in reserve with the 2nd Mounted Infantry, so I had only eighteen men left. About this time a heavy snowstorm came on, obscuring the Gurkhas, the guns, and the enemy from view.

ENTRANCE TO THE ZAMTUNG GORGE.

The Tibetans, to keep their spirits up, let off their jingals every now and then—goodness knows at what, as they could not see any of us, the fog was so thick, and even if they had, we were well out of range. About 12 noon the snowstorm abated, the fog lifted, and the sun began to struggle through. During the two hours' wait the force had become numbed with cold, and we were remarkably glad when the General told us to ride ahead and explore the defile. There was only one road, about six feet wide, to go along; down this we went in single file, about fifteen yards between the men, at a smart trot. No enemy was discovered, and we began to think what fools the Tibetans were. Then we came to where the defile opened out to about 150 yards, with the front blocked up by a precipitous hill covered with boulders. On we gaily went, and the leading man was just at the corner where the road and valley turn sharp to the left, when the whole of the hitherto silent, unanimated hillsides burst forth into flashes of fire and puffs of smoke. The Tibetans had concealed themselves splendidly, and had waited till we were within 150 yards of them, and could have allowed us to get within twenty if one of their men had not become excited and let off his gun too soon, which set them all going in front and both flanks and rear. There was nothing for it but to blow a whistle and signal the retire at the gallop, and off we went *ventre à terre.* This was the most extraordinary escape, as the Tibetans had numbers of modern rifles in addition to probably 1,000 matchlocks which were effective at that short range. My men said afterwards that the bullets were falling all round them, yet not a man or a pony was hit. I think it was owing to the extension between the men and to the pace at which we were going. It was very ignominious to be running away, but another whistle, which the men obeyed splendidly, pulled them up (it is a difficult thing to stop men sometimes when they are retreating at their best speed), and having got back about 500 yards they dismounted, packed their ponies under the cover of some old houses, and gave the enemy a taste of our bullets. They, seeing us retreat in an indecently hasty manner, were exultant, and, thinking we were defeated and had fled away for good, stood up and exposed themselves all over the hillsides. They sat down again in quick time when they found our Lee-Metford bullets buzzing in amongst them, and they evacuated the nearest sangar. In the midst of all this deafening row, a curious thing happened. Up on our left, 1,000 feet above us on a jutting-out rock, I saw standing a poor terrified female ovis ammon. Scared by the firing all round, she had taken refuge on this one solitary rock from which there was no advance.

BEFORE FIGHTING COMMENCED: TIBETAN SOLDIER WITH PRONG GUNS AT TUNA.

COLONEL YOUNGHUSBAND (R.) AND COLONEL HOGGE (L.) BEHIND.

We had carried out our instructions—viz., to find out where the enemy were down the defile, so I left the men where they were under cover, and rode back to report to the General. He in the meantime had ordered the 32nd Sikh Pioneers to move down the defile to cover us, and on the way back I found them extended advancing and eager for the fray, led by the gallant Captain Bethune, who was afterwards killed on May 6 at the first Karo Là fight. I reported to the General what we had found, and the Gurkhas having arrived on top of the spur far away to our left, outflanking and sweeping the Tibetan position, and the British Mountain Battery guns upon our right having opened fire across the valley over the heads of Colonel Younghusband and the General, the latter ordered the advance of the whole force. The Gurkha guns, Bubble and Squeak, carried by coolies, went down the defile at the double. Never had they gone so fast before, but fate had not decreed that they should bubble or squeak that day. I got back to my men just in time to catch up Captain Bethune's company, who were now committed to the attack. We galloped down the open defile, dismounted, and were just able to squeeze in on the left of the 32nd. We did not want much room, but still there was little room to be had. The Tibetan fire had diminished in volume and quality, owing to the fact that all the leaders and others armed with modern rifles had disgracefully deserted their men, and made good their escape, having had enough from a dozen or so Mounted Infantry rifles. Their men stuck to their position pluckily, and it was not till Captain Bethune's men had got within fifty yards of them and had fixed bayonets that they began to move off. Thanks to the splendid cover they had, I don't think more than twenty of them were killed amongst the rocks, but they were driven out of a magnificently strong natural position, with only one man wounded on our side. Immediately on their beginning to go, Captain Peterson and his Pathan company of Mounted Infantry, with whom I was glad to see my section of Mounted Infantry left in reserve, came clattering down the defile round the corner and after the fugitives. As soon as we could get hold of our ponies and mount, we joined up with Captain Peterson. The defile was passed and the ground had opened out, but was covered with huge boulders, behind which the Tibetans tried to make a stand and stop us; but what could they do, although there were about 1,500 of them? They were broken and flying, and we were advancing—about 150 Mounted Infantry—at full gallop, with the men making excellent practice, shooting from their ponies. About one and a half mile further on another valley ran in; the one to the right was the Gyantse road, down which only a few of the enemy had gone, cunningly enough, as they thought we were sure to go that way. The main body went up the valley to the left leading into the hills. Captain Peterson sent Lieutenant Bailey and one section down the Gyantse road, while he, seeing the way the rest of the Tibetans had gone, went up the left-hand valley with the remainder of the two companies of Mounted Infantry. Here the Tibetans had made another mistake. They had forgotten that the Gurkhas had climbed the heights which another portion of their force had occupied, and now the Gurkhas were coming down the other side of this spur into the valley up which the Tibetans were trying to escape, and thus helped to cut them off and capture them. The Mounted Infantry brought in large numbers of prisoners, amongst whom were many armed Lamas. My men captured 300 sheep and a quantity of yaks, ponies, and mules. Hundreds of matchlocks and swords were taken and broken up. Several Russian rifles (breech-loaders) and Lhasa-made Martini rifles were also found.

In the Mounted Infantry pursuit one of my native officers and one man were wounded, making the casualties of the force three wounded—an insignificant damage.

The road to Gyantse was now open, although there were many other strong positions on the road, including Naini monastery, which gave us a good deal of trouble later on.

On the morning of April 11 we got our first view of Gyantse Jong, monastery, and town, and although we were six miles from it, it looked a most formidable position to tackle, an impression which did not diminish on closer acquaintance. It stands on a rocky eminence about 400 feet high, which springs up out of the plain, and is only commanded by practically unscalable hills 2,000 yards off, quite out of range for Bubble and Squeak. The town lies round three sides of the base of this hillock, and on the fourth or north-western side is the monastery, surrounded by a fortified wall about thirty feet high. The plain is broad, open, well cultivated, and dotted all over with villages and groves of trees. What a relief to see trees again! They meant plenty of firewood, and comfort to the half-frozen force. The transport officers, and indeed everybody, were elated at the prospect of getting plenty of grain and forage for the animals.

The force camped on the right or Gyantse Jong bank of the river, about two miles from the jong. Both companies of Mounted Infantry were in front reconnoitring; but our orders were not to go into the town or bring on a conflict. The Chinese General Ma, stationed at Gyantse, and several Tibetan officials came out to meet us, and told us the place was unoccupied, and would be handed

THE CHINESE GENERAL MA AND HIS STAFF.

over next day. Numbers of Tibetan soldiers were seen flying at the top of their speed down the Shigatse road, and they were allowed to escape.

Next day, April 12, the force advanced to the jong prepared for any eventualities; but nothing happened, as, after the usual Tibetan delay and argument, two companies of the 32nd Sikh Pioneers under Captain Bethune marched through the town, up to the massive gates of the jong, which were opened to them, and then on till they reached the topmost storey, where the flag of England was hoisted, amidst mighty fattehs (cheers) from the Sikhs. Thus the strongest fortress in Tibet, and the one to which the Tibetans attach most sentiment and reliance, fell into the hands of the British without a shot being fired. This peaceful surrender was looked at by the force with mingled feelings of satisfaction and regret: regret because we had not had a decent hammer-and-tongs fight yet, and now it was considered that, Gyantse Jong having been given up, there would be little chance of it; satisfaction because it was felt that the Tibetans were afraid of the few hundred men assailing them. It was real luck for us that the Tibetans did not hold the jong then as they did later on. With practically no artillery, and such as we had certainly of no use against stone fortifications, with a very small force, and the extraordinary height and strength of the place, the capture of the jong, if held, would have been a most costly operation, even if the Tibetans only threw stones out of their numerous loopholes. It would not have done to suffer heavy losses amongst the men or officers, as there were no others to replace them along the 250 miles of communications, and there is no doubt the best political and military result was obtained in the peaceful surrender of the jong.

Gyantse stands strategically at the junction of three main roads of communication, which meet like the limbs of the letter Y much flattened out. The southern leg is the road we had come from Tuna and Chumbi; the western, down which the river flows, leads to Shigatse; the eastern, over the Karo Là pass, to Lhasa. It should be noted, in order to make clear the subsequent attack on the Karo Là, that from Ralung, at the foot of the Karo Là, some thirty miles along the right-hand branch, to Kangma, the same distance down the southern leg, stretches another track over the mountains past Niru, whereby a hostile force from Lhasa might evade Gyantse and attack the lines of communication.

Chung-Lo was the village selected for occupation by the Mission and escort. It suited the purpose well, as it stands on the right bank of Nyang Chu, or Gyantse river, where this is crossed by the stone bridge, and was very adaptable and strong for defence. It consists mainly of two

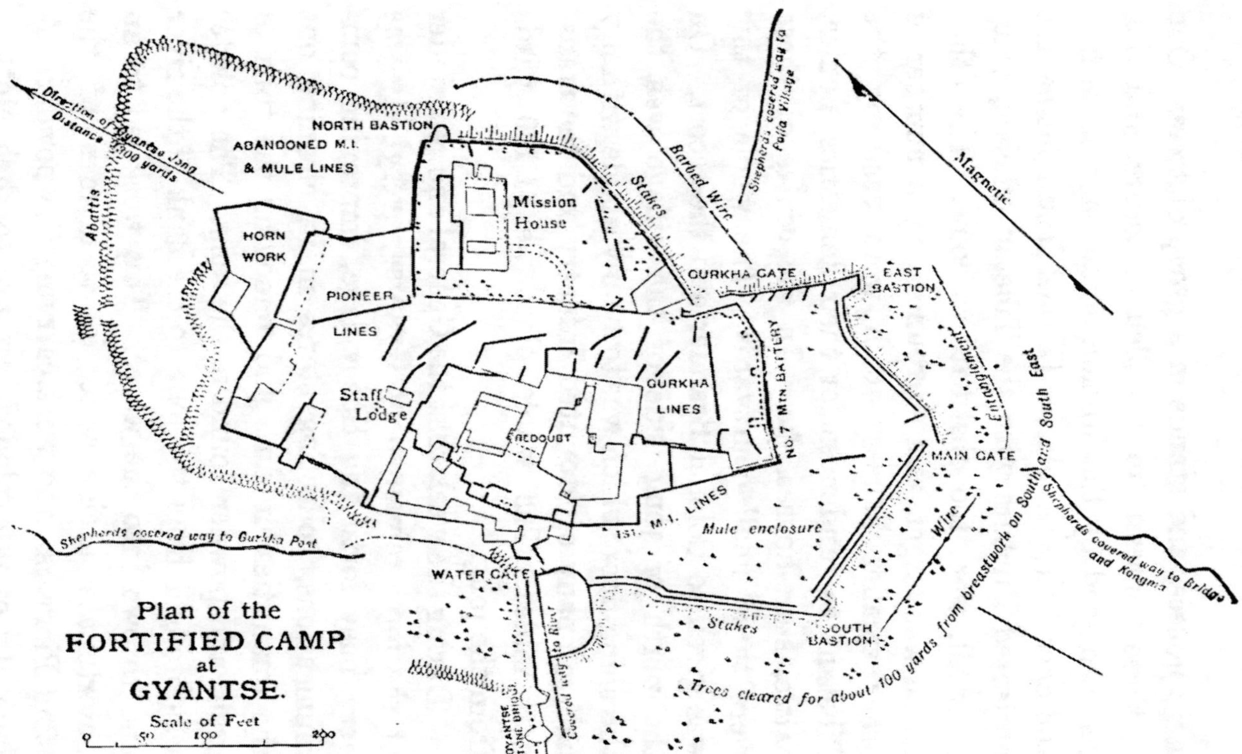
Plan of the
FORTIFIED CAMP
at
GYANTSE.
Scale of Feet
0 50 100 200
NORTH BASTION
ABANDONED M.I. & MULE LINES
Mission House
HORN WORK
PIONEER LINES
Staff Lodge
REDOUBT
GURKHA LINES
GURKHA GATE
EAST BASTION
No. 7 MTN. BATTERY
MAIN GATE
M.I. LINES
Mule enclosure
WATER GATE
SOUTH BASTION
Stakes
Barbed Wire
Magnetic
Abattis
Entanglement
Wire
Shepherds covered way to Palla Village
Shepherds covered way to Gurkha Post
Shepherds covered way to Bridge and Kongma
Covered way to River
GYANTSE STONE BRIDGE
Trees cleared for about 100 yards from breastwork on South and South East
Direction of Gyantse Jong Distance 800 yards

large houses, and stands in a grove of trees. One of these houses is in a walled enclosure, and this was occupied by the Mission on account of its fine audience hall suitable for Colonel Younghusband's projected Durbars with the Tibetan officials, who, after all, were too obstinate to come. The other house was larger, and surrounded by a number of other smaller houses which were used by the Tibetans as residences for their domestics, ponies, cattle, store-houses, &c. In the centre of these were three small courtyards. The whole of this was given to Colonel Brander and the escort. On the north or jong side of the village was the threshing-floor, which was to be my abode with my half-company of Mounted Infantry and the transport mules. The whole place was 1,100 yards from the jong.

During the week that the General and remainder of the force remained at Gyantse, everybody was very busy fortifying this village, improving communications, collecting stores in it, cleaning out the quantities of dirt and removing the tons of grain and powder found in the jong. The powder was brought from the jong to the bank of the river and thrown into the water. This work led to an unfortunate accident to fourteen men of the 32nd Pioneers, who were carrying the powder. A quantity of it exploded, set fire to their clothes, and burnt the poor fellows terribly. If they had not been on the bank of the river several of them would have been burnt to death; they saved themselves by jumping into the water.

A few days afterwards we heard of another sad explosion at Guru, where, in the same way, a native officer and some men of the 23rd Pioneers, and four out of my five Mounted Infantry men, were removing gunpowder from the house they were to occupy, when it exploded. The native officer, three Pioneers, and one Mounted Infantry man were killed, and the three other Mounted Infantry men were so badly injured that they had to be invalided, and one of them died. Lieutenant Maclean, attached to the 23rd Pioneers, and five Pioneers were also severely injured.

There were constant rumours that the enemy were collecting in various places some miles from Gyantse, which gave the Mounted Infantry a splendid opportunity of showing what use they could be. Every day was employed in reconnoitring in one or several directions up to twenty or twenty-five miles off. On the 13th we went to Gubshi, up the Lhasa road, at the junction of the Niru Chu and Ralung Chu, about eighteen miles from Gyantse. This is a place of great natural strength, but there was no enemy there then, although it was held afterwards.

On the way to Gubshi we heard from some Tibetans whom we met that there were still some of those who fought at Zamtung in front of us upon the road on their way to Lhasa. We gave chase, and came up with three Tibetan soldiers near Gubshi; these had their matchlocks still loaded, so we made them fire these at a mark 150 yards off, to see how they could shoot, and to our surprise they made very good practice. The rest of the enemy had passed through Gubshi early that morning, and were now beyond our reach. The three prisoners gave some useful information, were disarmed, and released next day, each being given three rupees, which surprised them very much, as from the rules of their own country they were quite sure that if they fell into our power they would lose their heads.

On the way back to Gyantse we came on the residence of the Rajah of Sikkim's fugitive eldest son. This young man, having disagreed with his father the Rajah, and also disliking the British Protectorate in Sikkim, fled to Tibet. As he would not return to Sikkim, the Rajah's second son was elected to the throne on his father's death. The fugitive son, on our visit, thought that the British were sure to punish him for his disobedience, and, indeed, believed that he would lose his head. He was therefore very much frightened when I told him that he had to accompany me at once to see Colonel Younghusband. His household made great lamentation, and his wife begged that he

TIBETAN WIFE OF THE RAJAH OF SIKKIM'S SON.

should be allowed to come in to Colonel Younghusband next day. This lady was a very handsome woman, and wore a most wonderful head-dress, about eighteen inches high, of the ordinary Tibetan shape, but covered with turquoises, pearls, and rubies, and worth at least 300*l*. I told her, through the interpreter, that nothing would happen to her husband, but that he had to come now. She, like a good wife, replied that he had not had his dinner, and that he could not go till he had it; but as this meal would take two hours, we settled the matter by his bringing his dinner with him. The Sepoys were quite elated at their capture, as they thought they had got nothing under a king, and this appealed to their way of thinking. Having been received by Colonel Younghusband, the exile was allowed to return to his home, but soon had to fly for his life and hide himself near Khamba Jong, on account of the threatening attitude assumed towards him by the Tibetans.

On the 18th we went to Dongtse, fifteen miles down the Shigatse road, the enemy being reported to have assembled there. This is a good-sized town, surrounded by a fine wall, and close to the hills. The whole place is commanded by a large and strong monastery on a steep spur just above the town. The place contained very fine houses and large stores of grain.

It was not held, and the inhabitants all came out to meet us, and agreed to our search of the town and monastery for arms, showing us all over the place, and proving very civil and well-disposed. They seemed to be the wealthiest Tibetans we had yet met, and well they might be, as they had a good climate, and the valley was very rich in cultivation, grain, grass, cattle, and sheep. This was where the Tibetan explorer, Serat Chandra Dass, stayed in 1882. We were in the house he occupied—a very fine one, too. The Lama who was his host was put to death, by order of the Lhasa authorities, for extending his hospitality to the Indian.

On the 19th General Macdonald and the force left Gyantse for Chumbi, to make preparations for a further advance to Lhasa, in case the Tibetans refused to negotiate at Gyantse.

CHAPTER VII

THE MISSION AND ESCORT AT GYANTSE—THE FIRST KARO LÀ FIGHT—ATTACK ON GYANTSE POST

It may be interesting to give the names of the Mission and escort officers, and the number of troops left at Chung Lo village at Gyantse.

The following are the officers of the Mission:

Colonel YOUNGHUSBAND, C.I.E.	British Commissioner
Mr. WILTON . . .	Chinese Consular Service
Captain O'CONNOR . .	Secretary to the Mission and Tibetan interpreter
Captain RYDER, R.E. .	Survey of India
Captain COWIE, R.E. .	Survey of India
Mr. HEYDON . . .	Geologist
Captain WALTON, I.M.S.	Mission Medical Officer and Naturalist
Colonel WADDELL, C.I.E.	P.M.O. of Force and Antiquarian and Collector of Buddhist knowledge and curios for the British Museum

Mr. Landon . . . 'Times' Correspondent
Mr. Newman . . . 'Pioneer' Correspondent

The following are the officers of the escort:

Staff

Captain Minogue, West Yorkshire Regiment (Staff Officer, Gyantse)

32nd Sikh Pioneers

Lieutenant-Colonel Brander (commanding at Gyantse)
Captain Bethune
Captain Cullen
Lieutenant Hodgson
Lieutenant Gurdon
Lieutenant Murray, I.M.S.

8th Gurkhas

Major Row
Major Murray
Lieutenant Coleridge
Lieutenant Lynch (Field Treasure Chest Officer or 'Money-bags')
Lieutenant Franklin, I.M.S.

Royal Garrison Artillery

Captain Luke (commanding seven-pounder guns, 8th Gurkhas)

1st Norfolk Regiment

Lieutenant Hadow (commanding Machine Gun Detachment)

1st Mounted Infantry

Captain Ottley (commanding 1st Mounted Infantry)

Hospitals

Major Wimberley, I.M.S. (commanding Native Field Hospital)

The troops consisted of four companies 32nd Sikh Pioneers, two companies 8th Gurkha Rifles, seventeen men of the 1st Norfolks, and half the 1st Mounted Infantry, altogether about 500 infantry and fifty mounted infantry, two seven-pounder guns, and two Maxims. It was thought that negotiations with the Tibetans were now sure to commence, and that there would be no more fighting, but the Tibetans proved themselves more dashing than that. Colonel Younghusband patiently waited, and invited the Amban and Tibetan delegates from Lhasa to visit him, but they never came.

The Chinese Amban's excuse was that the Tibetans would not give him transport, thereby admitting what little hold the Chinese had over the Tibetans, although they called themselves the suzerain power, which title the Tibetans allow them to retain as the Chinese pay well for it in cash and kind, and as long as the Chinese did not interfere with the internal affairs of state, they had no objection to the Amban and his 500 unarmed Chinese retainers remaining at Lhasa.

Now, the unfortunate Amban was in a sad plight, as he was looked upon by the British as the man to settle the difficulties with Tibet, but he could not even get transport to carry him, and was really living in fear and trembling at Lhasa, expecting to be attacked and murdered by the Tibetans any day. In fact, he was attacked in Lhasa in July, and several of his people killed.

The delegates could not come, as they were mostly in prison. The Dalai Lama and his 30,000 or 40,000 Lamas at Lhasa were furious when they heard the British had actually arrived at Gyantse and vented their wrath on the Tibetan National Assembly, imprisoning most of its members, including some of the four Shapés or Councillors of State. New ones were appointed, who were only renowned for their hostility to the British, and armies were ordered to assemble; so that while Colonel Younghusband was expecting negotiators to arrive at Gyantse, the Tibetans were evolving a very fine scheme to massacre and crush the Mission and escort there, then proceed down the lines of communication and wipe out our posts at various places, and finally attack Chumbi and drive out the remainder of our force there and capture the whole of Sikkim.

CAPTAIN RYDER, R.E.

At this time nothing was known at Gyantse about this scheme, and we settled down to what we thought was going to be a very humdrum sort of existence, the monotony of which was only broken into by pleasant trips of exploration and surveying with Captains Ryder and Cowie and Mr. Heydon.

These were very interesting, and in addition we used always to shoot something—a gazelle or two, a snow-cock, hares, duck, partridge, pigeons, and geese; in fact, anything good for the larder. There was a fishing contingent also, headed by Major Row, who used to keep us going with very good fish from the Gyantse River.

On April 21 Captains Ryder and Cowie, Mr. Heydon, and myself, with about twenty Mounted Infantry, reconnoitred the Yung Là, about twenty-three miles off, N.E. It was a long day, but we were well rewarded for our trouble, as we saw the Brahmaputra Valley at its junction with the Rong Chu Valley, as well as the two snow-peaks at either side of the Karo Là Pass. A good deal of absolutely new country was mapped that day.

On the 25th we made another excursion in the Khamba Jong direction, which was also profitable from a surveying and shooting point of view. I had been ordered to purchase as many ponies and mules as I could, and we picked up seven very good ponies that day; but as I could not carry sufficient rupees about with me to pay for them the owners were asked to ride them into Gyantse to be paid. This they readily agreed to. The Tibetan, when he rides, hardly ever moves off the road or path, which generally leads direct from one village to another, and although they are very fine riders along these paths, they are anything but such across country. We now took them at a smart canter straight across country, as being the shortest way home. At first the plain was quite level, and the Tibetans thoroughly enjoyed it, and vied with one another in showing off their ponies; but when it began to get dark, and the ground became rough, when jumps had to be negotiated, and their ponies, having become excited, began to pull, they became very nervous, and tried to pull up and walk. This we would not agree to at all, and told them that their ponies were evidently getting tired, and wanted whipping up from behind—a stimulus which the Sepoys applied with great glee, and off we went much faster than before. The Tibetans were terrified, dropped their reins and clasped their ponies round their necks, which drew roars of laughter and many gibes from the men. When we pulled up near Gyantse, they told us through the interpreter that they thought us wonderful riders; for our part we had a lot of fun out of them too.

The Mounted Infantry had plenty to do nowadays. They were out every day reconnoitring. Four men used to go daily half-way to Kangma to fetch the post—sixteen miles out and back, carrying up to 30 pounds (sometimes more) of mails on their saddles, and doing their journey nearly always in six hours. The post was now being carried by the 1st Mounted Infantry all the way from Tuna to Gyantse, a distance of about eighty miles.

The Tibetans were behaving very well at Gyantse, and were bringing in grain and fodder and all kinds of things for sale. They had established a daily bazaar near the post, where both men and officers bought what they wanted, whether eatables or curios. The poor people never had a better time, and never saw so many solid rupees before. Captain Parr, appointed by China to watch her interests, was living in Gyantse town near his friend General Ma. He had no escort, and did not suspect any hostile movement on the part of the Tibetans. General Ma, who must have known what was really going on, and was afterwards degraded by the Chinese, used to tell Captain Parr in a lordly way that he would not allow the Tibetans to make fools of themselves any further.

On the 26th a very unfortunate occurrence befell me. I fell ill, and was unable to do anything just when the opportunity for action arrived, for on the 27th Colonel Brander received information that the Tibetan army had collected at Ralung, about thirty-four miles up the Lhasa road and on the Karo Là Pass, which they had fortified and were holding in force.

If this report were true, the enemy were certainly threatening our lines of communication at Kangma, and Colonel Brander's orders were to guard the lines of communication and keep them open. He therefore decided to send out a reconnaissance of Mounted Infantry, supported by one company of the 32nd, to the Karo Là, and as I was too ill to go, Lieutenant Hodgson was put in charge. It was very sad for me to hear my own corps marching out and have to stay behind. Things were now so dull at Gyantse that to spend the time Colonel Brander began to teach me astronomy. The course was opened with the best intentions, but we never got beyond two lessons, as on May 1, in the middle of our lecture, a few Mounted Infantry orderlies rode in with a letter from Lieutenant Hodgson, reporting that the Karo Là was strongly held, that he had been fired on, and that he would arrive himself with his men next day. This was real stirring news, and Colonel Brander immediately decided to march to the Karo Là and oust the Tibetans. The weather had improved very considerably, although the whole country was covered with snow on the morning of May 1, yet that terrible excruciating cold was gone, and we felt warm in twenty-five or thirty degrees of frost.

Lieutenant Hodgson had experienced a very exciting time with the Tibetans. The people of

Ralung had assured him that there was no enemy on the Karo Là, and that they had never heard of a Tibetan army. Captains Ryder and Cowie and Mr. Heydon had accompanied him, and taking the Mounted Infantry from Ralung, they proceeded to reconnoitre the Karo Là. All went well till they got about two and a half miles beyond the summit of the pass, where they saw a great wall extending from the glacier on the right, down into the bed of the stream across the road, and finishing up in the perpendicular rocky side of the valley on the left. Although there was not a man to be seen, this wall made Lieutenant Hodgson suspicious. He could not tell whether it was an old or a new fortification, nor whether it was occupied or not, so he went forward with a few dismounted men, leaving the remainder of the half-company covering him. He got within 300 yards of the wall, when the Tibetans opened fire on him from every loophole. He with his men immediately lay down, and the Tibetans, thinking they were all killed, jumped up and exposed themselves, uttering triumphant war cries. At the same time showers of stones began to be thrown down by the Tibetans from sangars high up on the cliffs. A few volleys from the covering party behind soon made the Tibetans sit down behind their wall again, and enabled Lieutenant Hodgson to retire without a casualty except several bruises from stones.

He had done what was required of him, and from the enemy's fire he judged that they were very much better armed than those hitherto encountered. Their number he estimated at 3,000.

Colonel Brander's difficulty was transport, as he had not enough mules to carry rations for about 400 men for seven days, that being the time it would take to march to the Karo Là, fight a battle, and come back again. He therefore indented on the very friendly Gyantse Jongpen to hire him mules, donkeys, or ponies sufficient to carry 100 maunds. This was promised by the Tibetans immediately; but they had evidently been warned by emissaries from Lhasa not to help us with transport on any account, so they began to delay and make all sorts of excuses, till Colonel Brander could wait no longer, and ordered the Mounted Infantry out about 4 P.M. on May 1 to drive in all transport animals met with. The Mission also asked me to go to the Jongpen and send the old gentleman in to be talked to. As he had not complied with orders, he was to be kept in the post till the force should return from the Karo Là. This was the most fortunate thing that ever happened to the old man, as, had he been found by the Tibetans in Gyantse, when they occupied that place on May 5, they would most certainly have put him to a cruel death, as they did several persons who had intercourse with us.

The necessary transport having been collected, Colonel Brander marched out of Gyantse on May 3 for the Karo Là, with about 330 infantry, forty-five Mounted Infantry, two Norfolk Maxims, and the two Gurkha guns. The Mounted Infantry reconnoitred eight or ten miles in front of the column every day, and found out from the country people that the enemy were still at the Karo Là. This was very satisfactory, as it showed us that we were not doing our hard marching (sixteen miles a day) for nothing. Arriving at the Karo Là on May 5, Colonel Brander camped at the foot of the Kotal and glacier on the left, but pushed on himself, with all his commanding officers and the Mounted Infantry, to view the Tibetan position and make his plans for attack.

Cautiously creeping round a corner of the road from where the Tibetan wall was visible with the aid of glasses, we saw a few Tibetan soldiers moving about. They were there, and meant to fight us. The moment they saw us they concealed themselves behind the wall. The Colonel and all of us rode down the road to get a closer view, expecting to be fired at every minute, till we got within 500 yards; there we all dismounted, sat down, and had a good look at the position. Not a Tibetan showed anywhere, but we could see them moving occasionally behind their loopholes. This was a good instance of the necessity of blinding loopholes. So long as a man sat still behind a loophole, neither he nor the loophole could be seen, but when he moved away the light came through, and showed us that it had been occupied, disclosing also the position of that and many other loopholes.

There we sat for over an hour, but the Tibetans never fired a shot, hoping no doubt that we would go closer. Some officers were so tired out from marching up the stiff incline all the way from Gyantse, and wearied by the exhaustion brought on by these great altitudes (not less than 16,500 feet) and by the penetrating cold, that they lay down on the ground and went sound asleep, and had to be wakened up when it was time to go.

The Karo Là Pass is a defile about ten miles long, and 16,600 feet at its highest point, the heights at either side running up to well over 20,000 feet. For the first three miles it is very narrow, with very bad going up the bed of a frozen stream; it then opens out to about 600 yards across for another two and a half or three miles, where the Kotal is reached, decorated with Tibetan flags, streamers, and prayers. About one mile from the Kotal on the left a great glacier extends down to nearly the level of the road. In this huge blocks of ice are seen piled one on top of the other in promiscuous fashion. The whole of the left side is too steep to climb, and the right climbable with difficulty. The Kotal is broad and open, and on the other side the valley, falling gradually, opens out for about one and a half mile. Here another valley comes in from the right, and the main valley turns to the left and begins to get narrower again. On the right is an eternal snow-capped mountain, the lower slopes of which are very steep and shaly; the left side is almost precipitous and only accessible in places. Another mile and a half on, an under-feature runs out to the left from the mountain on the right, probably the result of a great landslip falling across and blocking up the valley. The stream has cut a narrow way for itself between this and the precipices on the left, across which passage the Tibetans had built their wall, about 900 yards long, extending along the top of the landslip. About 300 yards in front of this, on the right, was a large sangar flanking the road and sweeping the whole of the glacis in front of the wall, while near this numbers of stone-shoots were prepared. In the cliffs on the left were three sangars and several stone-shoots also flanking the road and about 600 yards in front of the wall. Behind the main wall is a dip in the ground about 200 yards across, down which runs the stream from another great glacier on the right, joining with the main stream. In this dip was the Tibetan camp, well concealed, and well protected from the interminable wind. Beyond the stream the ground rises again, forming another ridge running down from right to left. A wall was built on this also. On the left point of this ridge nearest the stream was a tower built to command the road and the narrow and deep bed of the stream. About half a mile further on, on the left bank of the stream, are the village of Zara and the Chinese post-house, the inhabitants of which must lead the coldest and dreariest existence. Hence the valley becomes more and more open till it is lost in the plain of the Yamdok Cho. A curious kind of scrub grows all through the defile, which makes not bad fuel. It does not grow in the open plains at either side of the pass.

It will now be understood what a prodigiously strong natural position the Tibetans held. They had chosen their sites for main wall, flanking sangars, and stone-shoots carefully and well. The valley was such that it compelled the attackers to advance at first on a narrow front exposed to fire from the 900 yards of wall, over a funnel-shaped piece of ground, where we were at the wrong or narrow end of the funnel. Their main wall could not be outflanked from our left owing to the precipitous cliffs capped with snow, and from our right it necessitated a climb of 2,000 to 3,000 feet to outflank it effectually. Their line of retreat was good, down a broadening valley into which ran many lateral valleys, affording them chances of escape.

Again, the cold and wind were so intense as to lessen considerably the fighting spirit of any foreign force, and the unaccustomed great altitude exhausted the men, though later on, when everybody got used to them, these high altitudes did not fatigue the force so much.

This was what Colonel Brander had to attack, with a force of under 400 rifles all told, and an enemy about 3,000 strong defending. On the morning of the 6th, before leaving camp to clear the Karo Là of the enemy, news came from Colonel Younghusband at Gyantse that after the departure of the expedition 1,600 Tibetans had attacked the post in the early morning of the 5th, but were repulsed with heavy loss by Major Murray and his little garrison of about 150 men, which included the sick, wounded, and fourteen men accidentally burnt in the powder explosion; that they retired into the jong, which they were now holding and fortifying. Another account of this surprise and the seizure of Gyantse Jong follows in Chapter VIII. Meantime, returning to the Karo Là operations, the orders for the attack were as follows: Major Row and his company of Gurkhas were to scale the heights on the left, and clear the enemy out of their sangars and stone-shoots. Captain Bethune with his company of the 32nd was to go down the bed of the stream and break through the wall across the bed of the stream and thus turn the enemy's right flank. I was to follow on his heels with the Mounted Infantry and to be ready to dash after the Tibetans immediately he carried the wall.

Captain Cullen with his company of the 32nd was to move along the glacis on our right, keeping as high up the slope as possible so as to endeavour to turn the enemy's left flank.

Colonel Brander and one company of the 32nd in reserve, the Norfolk Maxims, and the two Gurkha guns took up their position on a commanding plateau on the left bank of the stream, 1,100 yards from the wall.

At 9.30 A.M. the advance commenced, and the guns and Maxims were ready to open fire at 10 A.M. The Tibetans held their fire till we got to within about 600 yards, when one of them, losing control of himself, let off his rifle. This started them all off. Rifles, matchlocks, and jingals all rang out; the whole of the wall, and sangars on the right and left, were suddenly wreathed in smoke. Our Maxims promptly replied, and in this narrow defile, where every shot was echoed and re-echoed scores of times over, the roar of firearms was magnificent. We were quite safe marching down the bed of the stream, where we had good cover, and bullets from both sides were harmlessly passing over our heads. The bed of the stream bears to the left, and about 300 yards from the wall turns to the right. The right bank at this point is very steep and about thirty feet high. From the top of this bank or edge of the glacis, a large portion of the loopholed wall was only thirty yards away, but in the bed of the stream we were under cover from it. When Captain Bethune came to the corner, from which the wall is visible 300 yards off, he rapidly extended his men across the bed of the stream, where they laid down and opened fire, but it was quite futile, and the enemy behind their wall were perfectly safe. This wall was a work of art in fortifications; it was six feet high, built of large blocks of stone, and four feet thick. Behind each loophole it was chambered, so that the man firing through the loophole was screened from all but directly reverse fire. The enemy opened a heavy fire from all their loopholes, and at that close range a matchlock is nearly as good as a rifle. Several men were knocked over here, but Captain Bethune, recognising that it was yet impossible to take the wall by frontal attack, saved them by withdrawing them under cover of the right bank again, and at the same time sent me word to retire. The enemy in the sangars in the cliffs on the left which we had passed now turned their attention to us, and opened fire on our rear, but without effect, although

H 2

the bullets were falling all round the men. Captain Bethune signalled to me with his hand to retire still further, and this was the last time I saw that good soldier alive. He commenced retiring after me, and was last of all himself, when I suppose, chafing at not being able to breach the wall, and indignant at retiring, he took a few men with him, climbed the steep bank on to the glacis, and made straight for the wall above, where he and his bugler and one Sepoy, the first up, were all immediately killed.

Meanwhile the rest of us continued to retire, not knowing what took place behind, and having left the Mounted Infantry, two of whose ponies had been hit, well under cover, joined Colonel Brander to watch for the opportunity when we should be of use. The enemy's fire was so hot on the glacis, both from the wall in front and the sangar up on the right flank, that Captain Cullen and his few men could make no headway, but they lay down where they were and kept on peppering the loopholes. Several of these men were hit also. Major Row's Gurkhas on the left found they could make no impression on the sangars at their first attempt, as the loopholes were on the ground level, and the men in them could not be touched by any fire except that coming from the cliffs directly above them. The Gurkhas had therefore to retrace their steps till

THE FIRST FIGHT AT THE KARO LÀ.

A A. Main Tibetan Wall.
B. Tibetan Flanking Sangar.
C. 32nd Pioneers Attacking (Captain Cullen).
D. Section of 32nd Enfilading Sangar.
E. Tibetan Sangars on the left.
F. 8th Gurkhas Attacking Sangars.
G. Guns (Maxims), Reserve Co. 32nd, Colonel Brander and Staff.
H. 1st M.I. and Captain Bethune's Co. Retiring.
J. Hospitals and Transport.

they found a place up which they could climb, and get into a position whence they could hit the Tibetans in the sangar. The Maxim guns, although splendidly served and accurate, were useless against the wall. The range was too far for poor Bubble and Squeak, and although they fired over seventy rounds they only once hit their mark. The plateau on which Colonel Brander, his guns, Maxims, and reserve were posted was a very hot place, as the enemy's jingals and good rifles had the range of it thoroughly, and but for a dip in the ground the casualties here would have been very heavy. Throughout this fire Sergeant-Instructor Champion, who was in charge of the guns (Captain Luke having been too unwell to leave Gyantse), stood to them manfully, and worked them with the utmost vigour in the open without any cover, while the enemy's jingal bullets fell thick and fast around him, proving himself a credit to the Royal Regiment of Artillery.

At 1 P.M. the Gurkhas had got well above the sangar, and the lull in the fight was broken by their rifles ringing out in a brisk fire. It came as a complete surprise to the fifty odd Tibetans in the sangar, and as they were getting severe punishment, those who were not hit bolted out of the sangar to the rear along the single path. On these the reserve company of the 32nd and the Maxims opened fire, making them retreat all the faster. Some of them lost their footing and fell over the cliffs, a drop of 500 feet, and were smashed to atoms. Not one of them escaped; all were either killed or captured.

The capture of this sangar and the stone-shoots had no effect on the enemy's main position; in fact, it seemed to instil new life into them, and their fire was delivered with redoubled energy.

Colonel Brander therefore decided to send a section from the reserve under a native officer to climb the heights on the right and to enfilade the sangar on that side, which was sweeping the glacis and preventing Captain Cullen from getting near the main wall. This section had a long and trying climb of about 1,000 feet up a very steep shale slope, till they reached some crags through which they crept, hanging on for their lives, and got into a position about 500 yards from the sangar, in which there were about eighty of the enemy. At 2 P.M. the section of the 32nd opened fire, sweeping the sangar from end to end. The enemy bolted out, but being fired on by the attacking column too, soon bolted back again into the sangar; then, once more finding the fire of the 32nd section too accurate and destructive, they plucked up resolution and made another bolt, amidst a storm of bullets from the Maxims and the reserve company. The whole of the attacking column then made straight for the wall, but the Tibetans, seeing their sangars on the right and left abandoned by their own men, lost heart and fled. Now was the chance for the Mounted Infantry. Down the sharp-stoned and frozen bed of the stream they rode at full gallop, till the wall stopped them; they dismounted and spent ten minutes in breaking a hole in the wall to get through. Riding through the Tibetan camp, we only found a few stragglers, who were taken no notice of and left to be captured by the infantry coming up; but on reaching the top of the next ridge we saw the whole of the Tibetan army in one great mass in full retreat a mile and a half away, and carrying with them 500 men who were coming up to reinforce them. They were between two and three thousand in number. Down the steep incline went the men full pelt, and then along the open but hummocky valley at their best pace, till they got within 100 yards of their enemy, who tried to rally, but were scattered by the magazine fire delivered by those forty Mounted Infantry rifles. There were no horse-holders; every man as he dismounted, putting the reins on his right arm, knelt and fired. The Tibetans scattered in all directions, and then the Mounted Infantry, remounting, continued the pursuit, firing from their ponies. Wherever they saw a group of Tibetans trying to make a stand they went for them and dispersed them. At this work a pretty incident occurred: a Sepoy charged a group of Tibetans by himself, but they were too many for him and unhorsed him; a native officer came to the rescue, but his revolver jammed and would not go off, and he was unhorsed. Another Sepoy rushed up, but, fearing to fire lest he should hit either of his comrades, clubbed his rifle, smote the Tibetans with the stock, and kept them back till his comrades could get up and defend themselves, this Sepoy getting a sword-cut about nine inches long on his right arm.

The Tibetans having such a fine camp, we thought they must have good transport also, so on we pressed in order to capture it. About eight miles from the wall we came on a second camp of the Tibetans in a walled enclosure, who fired on us as we passed; but just then, catching sight of a lot of mounted Tibetans and transport a short way in front, we left the camp to be dealt with by the men following up, and continued after the mounted Tibetans, about twenty of them, and these, judging from their fine clothes, the leaders. These, as usual, seeing that the day was going against them, had left long before their own men, although all well armed with some kind of modern rifle, one fellow having a Lee-Metford rifle with fixed bayonet which had been taken from one of our men killed near the wall. They, thinking that their early start had put them out of our reach, were taking it easy. They were unpleasantly surprised when they found a few of the Mounted Infantry galloping in amongst them. One Tibetan, in trying to turn round on his pony and fire at us, shot himself dead. All but four were killed or taken, and the Lee-Metford recaptured. Having now reached the banks of the great lake, the Yamdok Cho, twelve miles from the wall, and no enemy being left in front, we started back as fast as possible, collecting all the ponies and transport animals we could, as the second Tibetan camp was still holding out. About twenty-five more Mounted Infantry had arrived and were engaging this camp, which they captured by charging straight at it. The enemy could not stand this, and hastily fled down the steep bank of the stream, which they crossed, waist deep, and made the best of their way up the Pekin road. A subadar and twelve men followed, inflicting heavy punishment and recapturing a second Lee-Metford rifle belonging to us. This camp was their store depot, as quantities of provisions, stores, ammunition, and tents were found, but as we could not carry them away they were burnt.

It was now 4.30 P.M., and we were ten or eleven miles from camp, which we reached at 9.30 P.M. It turned out to be the most trying march, one never to be forgotten. The men were worn out and hungry, as they had not time to eat their food, and the last they had taken was at 6 A.M. that day. The ponies were so done up that the men had to walk, and, what was worse still, a snow blizzard came on. It had been trying to snow several times during the day, and now it came down with unequalled fierceness, driving straight into our faces, and rendering the night pitch dark. The ponies could hardly keep on their feet, as the road was freezing hard and the snow made it as slippery as glass. One pony got paralysis and had to be shot, another died from exhaustion, several of the men collapsed and had to be put on their ponies and held there. It was most decidedly unpleasant, to say the least, and we were thankful when we got back to camp at 9.30 P.M., where, after a glass of rum all round and a glass from Colonel Younghusband's bottle of green chartreuse kindly kept for me by Colonel Brander, we began to think life was still worth living. The Mounted Infantry casualties were trifling—only three men wounded, two ponies killed, three wounded, one destroyed, one died; but we had done very well in the remount line that day, and had captured some very fine ponies and mules. The casualties in the force were Captain Bethune and four Sepoys killed and thirteen Sepoys wounded. The only sad recollection of a hard day and a good fight was the death

THE YAMDOK CHO.

of that fine soldier Captain Bethune, whose loss was felt and regretted by all who knew him.

In the absence of further reports from Gyantse, Colonel Brander, being anxious to send the garrison some help, and also to cheer them up with the news of the Karo Là victory, asked me if the Mounted Infantry were fit enough to march to Gyantse in one day. It was a forty-seven mile march. What a pleasure it was to be able to say yes! But in any case, fit or not, we would go; we were all ready to go anywhere so long as we got away from the inhospitable climate and fireless camp of the Karo Là.

We marched at 8.30 A.M. next day, accompanied by Mr. Landon of the 'Times,' who wanted to get his wire off with all haste, and Captain O'Connor. We had no baggage or kits; the men wore their poshteens and carried their Gilgit boots and one blanket on their saddles.

At Gubshi we halted for an hour, and as Captain O'Connor and Mr. Landon wanted to get on, sent them off with eighteen men, and they arrived in Gyantse at 5.45 P.M., having done their forty-seven miles in nine and a quarter hours, or about eight hours' actual marching—not bad for the Mounted Infantry after their five days' averaging thirty miles a day on half rations of fodder. The rest of us arrived a little later. Gyantse Post was a changed place, and so blocked up with abattis and all sorts of obstacles, that but for the friendly lantern held out by the Gurkha guard to guide us we should have had difficulty in finding the entrance. The kind-hearted Gurkhas gave me dinner, and as there was no other safe place we all slept in the mess-tent that night. We had lots to tell each other, and did not turn in till morning. They had had little rest since the 5th, as they had to be ready for another attack which they expected every night.

CHAPTER VIII

THE ATTACKS ON GYANTSE AND KANGMA POSTS, AND OPERATIONS AT GYANTSE TILL ARRIVAL OF RELIEVING FORCE

THE attack on Gyantse Post was delivered in the early morning of May 5 by 1,600 armed Tibetans. About 1,000 actually participated in the attack; the remainder, thinking the reoccupation of the jong, which was not held by our troops, of greater importance, went into the jong, making themselves comfortable there. The attack was quite unexpected by the garrison, no news of the Tibetan movements having leaked out, even to the Tibetan dooli-bearers and servants with the garrison. Several of these slept in Gyantse town that night, and were caught by the Tibetans and savagely murdered. Captain Parr blamed the Chinese General Ma very much for this, and considered that he must have been aware of the enemy's intentions, but refrained from giving any information to the British garrison for his own revengeful reasons.

Captain Parr and Ma, the Chinese General, had differences over political matters, Ma posing as the representative of the Amban, though never authorised by the latter, nor able to show any credentials. As Parr lived in Gyantse town, Ma, thinking it a good opportunity of letting Parr be murdered in order to get him out of his way, is supposed to have withheld information about the intended attack, of which he must have known if he had been a good Chinese official. He was afterwards dismissed from his appointment by the Amban. Parr had been an officer in a British regiment, and although now in the Chinese service, yet obtained two years' leave and served as a volunteer through the greater part of the South African War, and now, being fond of fighting, accompanied the force to the Karo Là on the 2nd. It was lucky for him that he had done so, as the Tibetans on their entry into Gyantse town on the morning of the 5th went straight for his house and sacked it, butchering his servants and all other inhabitants who were in the British service or gave them assistance, including my poor old interpreter. He was a Gurkha Newar who had lived at Gyantse for eighteen years and had adopted the Tibetan customs and dress. A piece of bad luck happened to him which cost him his life. A few days before we marched to the Karo Là he was badly bitten on the leg by a dog, and was therefore unable to accompany us. The morning of the attack was very dark, and the

Tibetans in their hide-soled boots crept noiselessly up to 100 yards from the post before they made their rush. The brunt of their attack was directed on the Mission walled enclosure, up to the very wall of which they pushed, and putting their guns and rifles through the loopholes fired vigorously. When Colonel Younghusband and the other officers of the Mission turned out they saw a circle of blazing fire from all the loopholes surrounding them. Fortunately the loopholes were too high from the ground on the outside for the Tibetans to depress their weapons sufficiently to hit anybody on the inside of the enclosure; all their bullets went high, whereby Colonel Younghusband and the other officers escaped being shot.

These officers in their various and peculiar night costumes—it was wonderful the number of pyjama strings that broke that night!—beat a hasty retreat into the garrison réduit; nothing else could be done, as they had only a couple of sentries with them in the enclosure. The Tibetans had also made their way into the Mounted Infantry and mule lines, but these were empty, as Major Murray had put the seven Mounted Infantry left behind in the réduit. The garrison were sharp at their posts and commenced a withering magazine fire on the enemy, which made them think how rash they had been.

The sick, wounded, and burnt men of the 32nd struggled out of hospital with their rifles, and to the best of their powers assisted in repelling the attack. When it got light enough to see clearly Major Murray ordered out three sortie parties, before whom the Tibetans withdrew to the jong, and were chased to the precincts of the town.

The Mounted Infantry men of their own accord saddled up and went out, and Major Murray said they did very good work. They told me afterwards that they had slain at least thousands of the enemy!

The losses of the garrison were only one follower killed, four Sepoys and one follower wounded; those of the enemy about 150 killed and 100 wounded. All the wounded found were dressed and looked after by Captain Walton; they healed up in a few days—a Lee-Metford bullet, unless it killed him outright, not seeming to have any very injurious effect on a burly Tibetan.

The foolish, misguided Tibetans had quietly assembled at Dongtse, twelve miles down the Shigatse road, with a view to putting into practice on Gyantse Post their historical plan of campaign—a night attack. Only about 2,500 of them had yet reached Dongtse, which they were making their commissariat store depot, by order of their

Quartermaster-General, the Ta Lama; but hearing that the greater part of the garrison had gone to the Karo Là, and feeling confident that Colonel Younghusband and the few with him would fall into their hands an easy prey, they did not wait for further levies to arrive, but sent off 1,600 men to wipe out Gyantse Post. These set out from Dongtse on the night of the 4th, marched all night, and, arriving at Gyantse a little before dawn on the 5th, attacked and were repulsed with loss.

The Tibetans immediately commenced fortifying the jong and mounting jingals. To everybody's amazement they opened fire on the post, and although the nearest points were 1,100 yards off, their fire reached and killed a follower in the post on the 7th. The Tibetans could be seen working like swarms of ants in the jong, and on the 8th Major Murray decided to disturb them in their work. He sent parties out to snipe them, and I was to go round to the other side of the jong and pepper them from that side. Just then a body of about thirty mounted Tibetans were seen riding out of Gyantse past Palla village, going up the Lhasa road. It was afterwards ascertained that these were going to meet their future spiritual and warlike leader, Dugdu Abor, a high Lama from Lhasa, who was arriving that day to take command of the Gyantse monastery. Now, it being dark the night before when the Mounted

Infantry arrived, they did not know that we had returned, and thought they were quite safe to go where they liked, even to march out in broad daylight, imagining the garrison were too weak to interfere.

Hastily getting twenty Mounted Infantry together, out I went, accompanied by Captain O'Connor, who, although a political officer, was always ready to join in a fight. We had got on to the Lhasa road between the Tibetans and the jong, thus cutting off their retreat, before they discovered us. When they saw us they quitted the road, and, turning to their left up the steep slope, galloped as hard as they could for a monastery at the foot of the inaccessible hills about one mile from the Lhasa road. It was hard luck not to have cut them off from that also, as we should have done, considering that we had the shortest way to go, but our poor ponies were spent, and could not even trot up the hill. Captain O'Connor, who was on a fresh pony, got a long way ahead of us, and blazed at them himself, hurrying them into the monastery. They copied our drill, and, dismounting, fired at us in excellent style, but forgot to hold their ponies. Three of these escaped and came over to us, and were captured. The monastery was too strong for us to attack, and, thinking our sally would be fruitless, we were about to return to the post when a rescuing party of about sixty Tibetans, all mounted, galloped out from the jong to help their comrades. The jong also opened a jingal fire on us. Leaving our ponies where they were under cover, we ran down the protected side of the spur towards the kopjes at the end. It was a race between the Tibetans and us who should get there first, and would probably have resulted in our both arriving on the kopje together if we had not taken advantage of the chance to try the fine target the Tibetans gave 1,000 yards off. It was the first time we put our new Lee-Enfield rifle to such a test, and we soon knew by the effect what a splendid weapon it is. The men opened magazine fire at 1,000 yards on the enemy, which stopped them, killing or wounding ten of them and several of their ponies, and sending the remainder flying back into the jong. The sharpshooters in Gyantse Post started firing on them also at 1,200 yards, and many more of them were hit before they got under shelter of the houses. Only about half a dozen of them reached the kopjes, which they occupied like Pathans ; but they were soon settled up with, four or five Mounted Infantry who had ridden round taking them in rear, while the rest of us tackled them in front.

This was the first and last cavalry action the Tibetans ever tried with us. We returned no casualties, but a native officer was injured in the eye by some gravel thrown up by a jingal ball, which hit the ground just in front of where he was lying down firing. This eye became worse, and eventually he had to be invalided back to India.

The effect of these reprisals on the Tibetans was like putting one's hand in a bees' nest, and they turned all their jingals and rifles on the post, and on us in our retirement, killing one follower in the post.

On the 9th Colonel Brander with his tired column arrived, and immediately began to make his preparations for the strengthening of the post, while Lieutenant Hadow kept the enemy busy with his Norfolk Maxims. On the 10th Colonel Brander made a reconnaissance in force up to the monastery at the foot of the hills, in which our opponents on the 8th took hasty refuge. It was not occupied yet, but was soon after.

From here a good view of the rear of the jong and monastery was obtained, which only showed what an impregnable place it was. A heavy fire was kept up by the Tibetans all day, which damaged some of the mules and Mounted Infantry ponies in their exposed camp. We abandoned this camp that night, and occupied a much safer place in the wood behind the post, which was to be our home for nearly two months.

The 11th brought another day's heavy firing from the jong. One of the Mounted Infantry ponies that went half-way to Kangma for the post

GYANTSE JONG AND MONASTERY, WITH PALLA VILLAGE ON THE RIGHT.

died on the road. On the 12th one man of the 32nd was severely wounded and one follower killed by the continuous fire from the jong. The fortifications in the post were going on splendidly under the able skill and indefatigable energy of Captain Ryder, assisted by Captain Cowie, and executed by large working parties, who had to work at night owing to the enemy's fire, making it harassing and arduous for the men. On the 13th we went down the left bank of the river along the left-hand branch of the Y, and burnt some villages within range of the post to prevent them being occupied by the enemy, and, as the garrison were very hard up for meat, brought in a lot of sheep and goats we found straying about. It was better that we should have them than the Tibetans. From the villagers we learned that large reinforcements for the jong from Lhasa and Khamba Jong would arrive next afternoon.

This excursion made the Tibetans very angry, and they turned all their jingals on us, making such good practice that we could not return by way of the bridge, but had to go up the river to the end of the wood, ford the river, and then get in under cover of the trees. This route became the only safe one to the post.

On the 14th we went down the left bank of the river again, hoping to intercept the reinforcements from Khamba Jong. About four miles down the river is Tsechen monastery, built on another precipitous hill about 600 feet high, about one mile long, and rising abruptly out of the plain—a very strong position. Some Tibetans told us—and swore to it by all their gods—that the monastery was unoccupied. We advanced in line, at ten paces extended, up to about 300 yards, when the monastery and hillside burst into flame and smoke; but, as usual, nearly all their bullets went high, and the others missed us. We had to retire sharp to a safer distance, from where our thirty rifles gave them a few rounds each. The place was occupied by at least 1,000 of the enemy, who cheered vociferously when they saw us retire. To show them that we knew what we were about, we burnt two of their villages and captured 250 sheep and goats, which drew from the jong another fusillade on the way into the post. The three men who were carrying the mail were fired on by a few Tibetans about eight miles out. The men let them have it back, and captured one of their transport ponies laden with barley-flour and their extra wardrobe. The mail escort was increased to eight men after this.

The 15th was only remarkable for a heavy fire from the jong, now an unceasing daily occurrence, and the advent of 'William,' which fired a ball 4½ pounds in weight up to 2,500 yards. This was the Tibetans' biggest gun, and on the first shot being fired they all stood up on their sangars and cheered. The sharpshooters and Maxims soon made them regret this outburst of exuberance.

On the 16th I went out with forty Mounted Infantry to meet Major Murray and his convoy of provisions returning from Kangma, whither he had gone on the 12th with all the available transport and 100 Gurkhas. As we were passing a village on the Lhasa road about one and a half mile from the junction of the Gyantse River with the Zamtung Gorge stream, we were fired on from the village. The men galloped straight for it, encountering an armed Lama close to the village. No information could be got out of the villagers until a couple of houses were burnt, and then they said that the Lama had come from the Naini monastery, and that they were all armed in the monastery, and intended to hold it in order to cut our road between Kangma and Gyantse. This would be a serious matter for us, so we went on to Naini village, where we met Major Murray and his convoy. The monastery was only 200 yards off, surrounded by a turreted wall thirty feet high—a very strong place. It was empty. The Lamas, having seen Major Murray arrive from one side and the Mounted Infantry from the other, took fright and fled.

As a precautionary measure we set fire to the main buildings as well as could be done without tools, and tried to weaken the defences as much as possible, but the place being so massively constructed it would have taken 200 men at least a month to destroy it.

On the 17th we all had a much-needed rest.

During the night of the 17th and 18th the enemy occupied a large house 400 yards away on the north-west side of the post, on the right bank of the river, and opened fire. The bullets from this house enfiladed the Mounted Infantry and transport lines, and soon three animals were wounded. At first we could not make out where the bullets were coming from, and, as there was the usual firing going on from the jong, thought they were coming from there. Colonel Brander determined to turn the enemy out of this house before they did any more damage, and ordered Bubble and Squeak to shell it. We were sent out on the left bank of the river to act as observation party of Bubble and Squeak's fire. The ground was too level and the range too far for these little guns, and they did not succeed in hitting the house. There were some other small villages on the left bank of the river within easy range of the post. These were now deserted by the inhabitants, and not yet occupied by the enemy, so we set fire to them in order to make them useless to the enemy, and then returned to the post by way of the ford at the east end of the wood, being unable, as usual, to cross the stone bridge owing to the fire of the enemy, who were particularly exasperated by the operations, and were firing all their jingals as fast as they could, and had the range of the bridge accurately. The path through the wood gave good cover, and the Mounted Infantry used to gallop in through this one by one, with fifty yards between the men; and during the two months' daily firing from the jong at the Mounted Infantry whenever they went in or out, not a single man or pony was hit, notwithstanding the jingal bullets falling all round them, which cut down branches from the trees, and sometimes hit the ground in front of a pony and threw up a lot of dust, making the pony shy and the man sit all the tighter. It was the best training-school imaginable for teaching mounted infantry how to ride, and it did make both Sikhs and Gurkhas into excellent riders. The men said one day that if bullets had been fired at them when they were learning to ride at Lingmathang they would all have passed out of the riding-school in three days. There is nothing like bullets.

As the guns were no help in the taking of the house occupied by the Tibetans, Colonel Brander determined to make a night attack, breaching the house with guncotton and then storming it. The attack was ordered for the morning of the 19th at 3 o'clock, and was to be carried out by one company Gurkhas, under Major Murray, as storming party; one company 32nd, under Lieutenant Hodgson, who were to take up a position beyond the house to cut off the enemy's retreat; one company 32nd, under Lieutenant Mitchell, in reserve; and the explosive party of the 32nd, under Lieutenant Gurdon. Noiselessly they crept out of the post in the dark, and got within fifty yards of the house before the Tibetans were aware of their approach. Only a few shots were fired by the Tibetans before Lieutenant Gurdon, with his men, rushed up and laid their guncotton against the door. Lieutenant Gurdon lit the fuse with his lighted cigar; a few seconds, and the charge exploded with a tremendous bang, shattering the door and bringing down large pieces of the wall at both sides. Instantly Major Murray and his Gurkhas charged into the house, and the place was taken. Those Tibetans who remained were either killed or captured, and those who escaped from the house met the same fate at the hands of Lieutenant Hodgson and his men. They lost about fifty in killed, wounded, and captured, and our loss was only three men wounded. There were several others, including Major Murray, who were hit with bricks and stones, hurting them severely; but only bullet-wounds or sword-cuts were considered fair wounds and returned as casualties.

This was a little affair, but could not have been

better executed, as the casualty list shows. It was not a case of superior weapons, as the attacking column never fired a shot till the house was taken, where the Tibetans were met on equal ground, and this complete success was obtained by the celerity, determination, and dash of the attacking column. Fifty Gurkhas, under Jemadar Mewa Thapa, were left as a permanent garrison, and the place was put into a state of defence, and henceforth known as the Gurkha Post; and thus ended a most successful morning. The guncotton explosion thoroughly woke up the people in the jong and town, who, thinking they were being attacked themselves, started up, and commenced a tremendous fire. Their jingal fire was all directed at the post, most probably because the jingals were trained that way, and, it being dark, they did not know where to alter them. The whole face of the jong, rock, monastery, and town were lit up with the flashes from thousands of matchlocks, Lhasa Martinis, and jingals. It looked very pretty, and was the finest display of fireworks most of us had ever seen, eclipsing even those of the Delhi Durbar. It was perfectly harmless, of course, and the enemy not only wasted quantities of their powder and shot, but gave the first opportunity of realising and estimating the number of armed Tibetans occupying the jong. Local information put the numbers at 7,000, and from this voluminous display of fire one was inclined to believe that the information was correct. During the day a man in the 32nd was severely wounded by a rifle bullet fired from the jong, and Major Wimberley's medical pannier, which he had put out to air in the sun, was smashed to pieces by a jingal ball, which gave rise to many remarks about observing the terms of the Geneva Convention.

The day had something more in store for us still. About four in the afternoon I was sitting in Captain O'Connor's room when in rushed his tame Lama—who interpreted for him—in a state of great excitement, and gabbled something in Tibetan, which, being translated by Captain O'Connor, was that the Tibetans had hung up the Mounted Infantry mail escort a short distance from the post, and were shooting at them. We rushed down to the Mounted Infantry lines as fast as possible, and found that Colonel Brander, who had got the news first, had already ordered the men to saddle up. My own pony was ready, so out we bundled through the wood, accompanied by Lieutenant Hodgson and a sporting doctor, Lieutenant Ellias, I.M.S., both keen on seeing a fight. About a mile from the end of the wood up the river is a large thicket on both banks, and numbers of small villages are dotted about for three or four miles up the river.

The Tibetans in the early morning occupied all

these villages, and fortified and mounted jingals in one large village on the right bank about 1,000 yards from the river.

The Mounted Infantry mail escort on their way back to Gyantse were passing between one of these villages and the thicket on the left bank of the river, when the Tibetans, having cleverly ambuscaded them, opened fire from all sides. One man and five ponies were killed on the spot, the Lance-Naick in command was hit through both arms, rendering him useless, another man was wounded in both legs and could not stand up, and two out of the remaining three ponies were so severely wounded that they had to be destroyed afterwards. The Tibetans got so close that they used their swords on the ponies. The Lance-Naick got his men together in the thicket, whence they retaliated on the Tibetans, and shot them down so quickly that they drew off a bit, though still keeping up a steady fire on them. The Lance-Naick behaved most gallantly, and although unable to use his rifle, opened the packets of cartridges with his teeth and passed them round to his men to fire. The wounded man crawled behind a tree, whence he kept up a vigorous fire on the enemy; and thus, true to their duty, they defended the mail-bags on their killed and wounded ponies so successfully that out of the seven mail-bags in their charge only one fell into the hands of the enemy, as well as two saddles and bridles and one rifle.

Quite 1,000 Tibetans were on the move in the thicket and villages when we arrived near the scene. Subadar Sangat Singh, with fifteen men, went up the right bank of the river, and the rest of us, with about twenty men, went along the left bank. The Tibetans, seeing the tables were turned, on feeling our heavy fire began to make themselves scarce. They were driven out of two villages and the thicket on the left bank, only to be caught by the Subadar and his men coming up the right bank. There was no rest for them now, and they began to scatter and hide themselves where they could. About twenty or thirty of them, being hard pressed, took up a position in a large house with a parapeted roof made of sods and brushwood and started firing, as they intended to give battle. The challenge was accepted at once, and the attack commenced. We got up under the walls without anyone being hit, thanks to the large interval between the men. There was only one door to the house, and we could not get in that way as they were shooting out of it really well. Lieutenant Hodgson and four or five men looked after the door, and with their bayonets made a hole in the wall and fired into the house, while the rest set fire to the brushwood on the roof, and went round the house to try to break an entrance. A small hole was found in the wall, and as a Sepoy went up to it a Tibetan made a vigorous sword-thrust at him through the hole, and just missed him. The Sepoy put his rifle-barrel into the hole and commenced magazine fire, which must have been very unpleasant for those inside. As the walls were too substantial to break through, the next thing was to get on to the roof, and fire was commenced from that elevated position into the house, the enemy returning it. Their nerves were beginning to get shaky, and four of them bolted out of the house by the door. These, however, had to run the gauntlet of our fire, which deterred the others from coming out. The men were being collected on the roof to jump down into the open space inside the house, when orders were received from Colonel Brander to retire as it was growing late and darkness was falling. Just at that moment about 500 more Tibetans were seen collecting in the hills some distance off. Much to the regret of all we had to leave our job unfinished and return to the post.

Relying on our ponies to get away sharp, we stayed as long as possible, and to our surprise, when we did want to go, we found that the dismounted mail escort had followed us up on foot, including the two wounded men, who had walked and crawled along for about two miles. The affair now became a rear-guard action, the body of

Tibetans in the hills having come on. Lieutenant Ellias put one of the wounded men on his own horse, and took him back to the post himself. The other was put on a pony, and, being held there by two men, was taken in, covered by the remainder of the men, who had to deliver a hot fire to keep the Tibetans off. We arrived at the post as it got dark without further casualties.

It will be seen that this had been a very busy day. Our casualties for the day were one killed and six wounded, including one of the 32nd men hit in the post by fire from the jong, five ponies killed, and two wounded. This was quite the sharpest affair we had had so far, but it only made the men all the keener to try conclusions with the Tibetans. It also showed that the Tibetans had occupied all the villages for miles up the river, and that they intended to stop our daily mail and cut our communications.

On hearing how the Tibetans had disposed themselves in the villages, Colonel Brander issued his orders for their expulsion next day. He had no idea of allowing the mail to be stopped for a single day, and sent us out at three next morning to escort the mails half way on their journey, and to see if Naini monastery was held. Having done this, we were to cross the river six miles up, and come down the right bank so as to catch the Tibetans on the plain when he had driven them out of the villages. We were to be in position here by 9 A.M.

Naini was not occupied, but the villages on the right bank were, particularly the large fortified one. We took up our position about 1,200 yards from this, near the Lhasa road, as much under cover as possible; but the enemy in the house had sighted us, and showed us that they had good rifles, as their bullets were dropping on every side. There were some men in the thicket on the other bank of the river 2,000 yards away. These opened on our rear with Mausers or Lee-Metfords, or some small-bore rifles, as their bullets, which arrived before the report was heard, kept just going over us. The place we occupied afforded the best cover for the ponies, and was the best position for us, so we had to stay there. Colonel Brander with his column soon appeared, and commenced on the small villages. The enemy fled from the first three, which were burnt and destroyed, and took refuge in the big village. In the fourth village, Thagu, which was one big, solidly built house, the enemy made a stand. Lieutenant Gurdon, with his explosive party, immediately went forward, and, although he and his men had to take cover in a pond of water at one time, succeeded in laying his charge and blowing a breach. Lieutenant Hodgson charged in with his men, and the house was taken, Lieutenant Hodgson receiving a severe sword-cut in his arm which put him *hors de combat* for a fortnight. The big village still remained, and Colonel Brander, having rested his men, prepared to advance against it. The people in the jong were getting very excited and threatening, so Colonel Brander sent us a message to move round on his left flank to keep off any people coming out from the jong.

The attack on the house now developed, and from the enemy's fire it could be seen that it would be a difficult and costly operation. There was no cover, and the men had to advance across the open; and well they did it, getting only one man killed (1,000 yards range) and two wounded. They had got up to the wood and garden walls surrounding the house when Colonel Brander got a message to say that the jong people were meditating an attack on the Mission in the post. Of course he had to think of the Mission first of all, and had therefore to withdraw his attack on the fortified village and retire to the post, sending ahead the Mounted Infantry, including the eight Norfolk Maxim-gun men, right good fellows, who, mounted on ponies belonging to officers of the Mission, volunteered to join us that day. The Tibetans in the jong, seeing the column returning, thought better of their attack on the post, and contented themselves by firing all their jingals on the column coming back. The casualties for the day were two men of the 32nd killed, Lieutenant Hodgson and three men badly wounded.

In the afternoon we went out again to meet the mail escort. They reported all quiet along the road, but that there was a gathering of the enemy on the Ralung-Kangma cross-road (see p. 76). There were no signs of Tibetans in the villages which were attacked that morning, but they were still in the fortified house and village, and fired a few jingal-shots at us.

The 21st was a fairly quiet day till the afternoon, when they renewed the fire from the jong, and also from Palla village, on the right front of the Mission enclosure, 800 yards off. They had been busy all day mounting jingals in this village, and also behind a large garden wall between Palla and the jong. They loopholed the whole of this wall, thus extending their front on our right flank.

Reinforcements were to arrive at Kangma on the 23rd, consisting of the section No. 7 British Mountain Battery, under Captain Easton and his subaltern, Lieutenant Bennett, about eighty of the 1st Sappers and Miners, under Captain Shepherd, D.S.O., with Lieutenants Garstin and Walker, about fifty of the 32nd Sikh Pioneers, under Major Peterson, D.S.O., and Lieutenant Mitchell, and the Gurkha section of the 1st Mounted Infantry. I was very pleased when the General ordered these up, as they had put in a very hard, cold, wearisome time with the yak transport, in which duty, Captain Tillard, D.S.O., General of the Yak Division, said, they had acquitted themselves well, and were first-rate at scouring the country and bringing in yaks to replace those that died. We had not seen them either for about two months, and now looked forward to a pleasant meeting.

These reinforcements were very welcome in Gyantse, as the little garrison had lost up to now in killed and wounded fifty-six, and about another fifty were unfit for duty. Then fifty Gurkhas were in the Gurkha Post, so that out of the original 550 only 294 were left to defend the post and make reprisals, while the enemy were steadily increasing, and now numbered about 12,000 in and around Gyantse. Our men were beginning to feel the hard work, as the guard duties were very heavy, and all the defensive works which entailed fatiguing labour had to be carried out at night, so that the whole garrison had had only one or two nights in bed for the past fortnight.

The fifty-four Mounted Infantry had lost six in killed and wounded, and three unfit for duty; the remainder had had a very hard time of it, and consequently the Gurkha section of twenty men would be well received. To bring these reinforcements in Colonel Brander despatched 300 mules, escorted by forty-three Mounted Infantry and fifty men of the 32nd Pioneers with Lieutenant Mitchell, to march to Kangma in one day, thirty-two miles. The men of the 32nd we mounted on the mules. The mule pack-saddle is a poor thing to ride on, and most uncomfortable, but by putting the men's and drivers' wadded quilts (rezais) on the saddle, they could sit them all right.

We started at 2.30 A.M. on the 22nd, and as it was pitch dark, and there was only one road of exit through the parapet and wire entanglements, it took an hour and a half to get all the mules out; but by the time the Tibetans fired their reveille gun the mules were well out of range from the jong, and on their way. The main object was to get those mules to Kangma without mishap, and as the road passed through the village of Naini, and within 200 yards of the monastery, a place bound to be occupied by the enemy, we crossed the river and passed Naini on the far bank of the river. It was lucky for us we did, for no sooner had the centre of the convoy got level with the village and monastery than the Tibetans opened fire on us, showing that at last they had occupied it. Five hundred Tibetans had entered the monastery the night before, and were determined to cut up any of our small parties passing along the road through the village. They forgot we could go along the other side of the river. We got through all right with only one mule-driver wounded, having peppered any Tibetans who were unguarded enough to show themselves on the monastery walls, and arrived at Kangma without further incident, where we found Major Peterson with the reinforcements.

The next day we marched to Churria, half-way to Gyantse, and the following day, the 24th, arrived in Gyantse. The enemy at Naini fired on us again, but this time they did not get off so easily, as they received a nasty fire in return, and the guns fired two shells, which found their billets and did good execution. This was an instance of using shrapnel as common shell. The Mounted Infantry meantime got on an eminence from which a portion of the interior of the monastery could be swept with fire. This combined effort resulted in the enemy ceasing fire. Doubtless they regretted having begun. They evacuated Naini that night, and came into Palla village. They were mostly men from Kham, 800 miles east of Lhasa, who bore a great reputation as fighters, but, being mercenaries, proved themselves better robbers of the Tibetans than fighters in their cause.

The 25th was only remarkable for the heavy fire from the jong, and from Palla village, where the enemy had mounted some very good jingals, and had some good rifles also. In fact, their matchlocks were making themselves felt, as the village brought them just in range. Palla village being on their right front, they were enfilading the battery-mule lines at the right rear of the post, and one mule was killed before the animals were put in a safer place, and protection built for them.

The Mounted Infantry spent the day in making room for the Gurkha section in the already crowded lines, and improving our parapet. All the new-comers were occupied in clearing and fortifying their respective positions, while Colonel Brander drew up his scheme and issued his orders for the attack on Palla village next morning. At 3 A.M. on the 26th the Palla village attacking column marched out of the post, consisting of the two 10-pounder guns, Bubble and Squeak, one Norfolk Maxim, the Sappers and Miners, two companies 32nd Pioneers, and one company 8th Gurkhas.

The Gurkhas, guns, and Maxim were placed in reserve on the kopje about 800 yards north of Palla, the scene of our cavalry action. The attack was delivered from the north in three columns. One company of the 32nd, under Major Peterson, D.S.O., attacked the right of the village; one company 32nd, under Lieutenant Gurdon, attacked the centre; and the Sappers and Miners, under Captain Shepherd, D.S.O., attacked the left. With each column was an explosive party. About 4 A.M. a few shots were fired on both sides, and a few minutes afterwards one charge of guncotton went off with a tremendous bang. This had been laid by Captain Shepherd's detachment. The Tibetans were now thoroughly wakened up in the jong and in the village, and we in the post were treated to another display of fireworks; as usual, their jingals being directed on the post, we got the benefit of it.

About half an hour later another charge of guncotton went off, and after this there was a decided lull in the enemy's firing, and we in the post thought it was all over. Day now began to dawn, and with the increasing light the Tibetans increased their fire, and we could see what was going on. Major Peterson's column had got into the outer enclosures of the village, and in front was the main wall of what was known as the palace, thirty feet high, and not a doorway in it to blow in, with the parapet on top manned by Tibetans, who were shooting away for all they were worth. The other two columns had each forced an entry into a house, the occupants of which, to their everlasting credit, fought magnificently, and would not be taken prisoners. About 6 A.M. another charge of guncotton went off and another house had fallen to the Sappers. There were two large houses in the centre of the village, one known as the 'three-decker,' as it had three storeys, and another house on the left flank of the village, still strongly held by several hundred Tibetans, who were making so good a resistance that the explosive parties could not get near them. It was in endeavouring to do so that Lieutenant Garstin, R.E., was killed, and Lieutenant Mitchell, 32nd, wounded, besides five or six men killed and wounded. Also Captain O'Connor, R.A., the Secretary of the Mission, who, laying aside his pen for the sword, was in the thick of it, was severely wounded. The Sappers had got into the house nearest the jong, and for a long time could not get at the Tibetans in the upper storey.

Meanwhile the ten-pounders and Maxim, the Gurkhas and the sharpshooters in the post kept up a dropping fire on the jong to prevent the occupants from firing at the attacking columns in Palla. This was not very effective, as the Tibetan fortifications in the jong were too well built to be affected by shrapnel or rifle fire, and the range was too far for Bubble and Squeak's double shell. The Pioneers and Sappers were slowly blasting and sapping ways through the houses they had already got, up to the three-decker, and matters seemed to come more or less to a standstill, when about noon the Tibetans endeavoured to reinforce their comrades in Palla from the jong. About forty mounted Tibetans, accompanied by some men on foot, dashed out from the jong across the 600 or 700 yards of open space. It was a forlorn hope and a brilliant one. A feeling of admiration for the Tibetans thrilled through all ranks who saw their gallant effort, which, of course, was doomed to failure, although supported by every rifle and jingal in the jong. Lieutenant Hadow with his Maxim and the Gurkha reserve company opened fire on them on one side, and the other Norfolk Maxim and the sharpshooters in the post took them on the other, and although the range was over 1,000 yards, in less time than it takes to tell it those not put *hors de combat* had made their escape. On their failure the enemy on the roof of the house nearest the jong lost heart, and began to make good their escape by jumping down, and wriggling along the ground on their stomachs. This house was soon cleared, but the three-decker and the other house still held out as gallantly as ever till about 1 P.M., when Colonel Brander ordered Captain Luke to try what he could do with Bubble and Squeak. To the astonishment of everybody, Bubble and Squeak, firing from the high ground where they were, dropped their large double shells with the utmost precision on the tops of these two houses, and breaking through the roofs, set them on fire. The poor Tibetans had to bolt out of them now, and at 2 P.M. Palla was captured. Over 150 men were made prisoners. These were of the greatest use to Captain Shepherd afterwards in digging the covered ways between Palla and the post, the Gurkha Post and the post, and from the post through the wood, besides being employed on any necessary sanitation or fortification works. They became splendid workmen, including the Lamas, several of whom were captured, and finding they were not ill-treated or ill-fed, they became perfectly happy and contented, cheerful, merry souls, and declared that they had a much better time as prisoners in the hands of the British than as soldiers with the Tibetans. There were 500 Tibetans in Palla, and their losses in killed, wounded, and prisoners were very heavy. Our losses were Lieutenant Garstin and three Pioneers killed, Captain O'Connor, Lieutenant Mitchell, and Lieutenant Walker severely wounded, and nine men all dangerously wounded.

Immediately Palla was captured steps were taken to put it in a state of defence and garrison it with one company 32nd Pioneers under Subadar Sher Singh.

The effect of the capture of Palla on the Tibetans was serious, as it blocked the Lhasa road and prevented them getting water from a pond on the north-east side of the town, so that the only road of supply open to them now was the Shigatse road, and in that direction also they had to get their water. Accordingly, on the evening of the 27th a large convoy was seen coming along the Shigatse road for the jong. We were ordered out to capture them if possible. The ponies, having had a day's rest the day before, were quite fresh, and galloped down the left bank of the river in good form. The river was now beginning to rise, and it was difficult crossing, many of the ponies having to swim. The convoy, seeing us crossing the river, made the best of their way into a defended village, but were caught in a smart fire from the Mounted Infantry, which caused a good deal of confusion amongst them; loads were thrown, and the whole convoy scattered into the hills, and we got two very good ponies belonging to the escort.

That night we buried poor Garstin. The funeral was fixed for 5 P.M., but the fire from the jong was so heavy that it was considered an unnecessary risk to take the men and officers outside the post while it continued. The burial accordingly took place at 9 P.M. by the light of the moon. Silently and sadly the men fell in, and marched out of the post to line the path to the cemetery on the river bank where Captain Bethune was buried. Lieutenant Garstin was carried to his grave and laid to rest by four of his brother officers of the Royal Engineers, adding one more to the long roll of officers of that splendid corps who have met their death doing their duty on the battlefield. Colonel Younghusband, in his deep sympathetic voice, read the Burial Service, and though there were no three volleys fired nor Dead March played nor Last Post sounded, yet it was the most touching soldier's funeral that any of those present had ever seen.

On the 28th Captain Cullen, with 100 of the 32nd Pioneers and fifty of the Mounted Infantry, escorted all the mules to Kangma in one day to bring up a convoy from there. Major Peterson and a force accompanied us to Naini monastery, again thinking it might oppose us. The Tibetans had abandoned it, however, and Captain Shepherd blew down portions of the front walls, and made it as untenable as possible in the time available. On the way back to Gyantse he destroyed several small villages which were a constant menace to the mail escort.

On the night of the 29th the Tibetans were afoot in large numbers, and made a show of attacking the post at Gyantse. They contented themselves by occupying the partially destroyed villages on the left bank of the river, and the wood, whence they fired at the post for about two hours, shouting and yelling like fiends let loose from below; and having satisfied themselves that they had done enough for that night, withdrew into the jong. The only harm they did was to disturb the garrison's sleep and keep them standing to arms half the night.

We returned to Gyantse from Kangma, arriving

on June 1. Naini monastery was empty, and the Chinamen in charge of the Chinese mails said that one of the two shrapnel shells fired on the 24th killed three Tibetans in the monastery, amongst whom was one of their generals, and that they were ordered that evening to leave Naini monastery and occupy Palla village, which they did, and were probably sorry for the exchange. They were, as already said, 500 men from the Kham country.

Colonel Younghusband sent a letter into the jong by a Tibetan prisoner under a flag of truce, to which the Tibetans made their usual reply—that no negotiations could be carried on until the Mission and escort retired to Yatung. Colonel Younghusband replied that as he was now present in Gyantse he was ready to meet the Tibetan officials there, and that he could not think of putting them to the trouble and inconvenience of coming to Yatung, so long a march. There was no reply to this, and there was no firing from the jong all that day and all the next, nor on our side either. The prisoner who did messenger, instead of making good his escape, as he might have done, returned to the post after delivering his last message.

The next day the Tibetans remained very quiet, and as we did not fire on them they took this opportunity to strengthen their fortifications.

To prevent this, about six o'clock in the evening a message was sent to them by the same prisoner that if they did not recommence fighting earlier fire would be opened on them. They did not do anything until that night. The prisoner returned to the post again. The Mounted Infantry were out reconnoitring up the Lhasa road all day, and found that the Tibetans had evacuated all the villages they had held on the right bank of the river, and were informed that about 4,000 more Tibetans had assembled at Gubshi, and that the Karo Là was again held and being strongly fortified.

About 12.30 on the morning of the 3rd the Tibetans commenced another attack on the post, surrounding it and Palla village. They never came closer to the post than 600 yards, but large numbers of them closed in on Palla, and the garrison opening fire killed twelve of them.

They drew off about 4 A.M., and we all went to bed again. The Tibetans were very busy all day and fired a lot of lead, which kept crashing through the trees in the Mission enclosure, and annoyed everybody very much. They wounded one sapper and one mule returning from work at Palla village.

A very unfortunate thing happened to me this day. I had cut my hand a few days before in making a loophole in a ruined wall. The cut seemed nothing at the time, but now blood-poisoning had set in, and the whole of the right arm was swollen and useless. It was most annoying, and the pain was so great I could not get about, but thanks to the kind care of Major Wimberley and Lieutenant Ellias, who burnt the wound with pure carbolic acid, I was all right and fit for duty in a week; but it did me out of being present with the company of Mounted Infantry in the enemy's attack on Kangma. On the 4th the fire from the jong wounded a sapper in the post, killed Lieutenant Gurdon's pony, and wounded one battery and two transport mules. On the 5th Mr. Tulloch, superintendent of post offices, came to stay for a few days. He had hardly arrived in the post when the Tibetans in the jong shot his pony. This made him very anxious as to how he would get away from Gyantse again, as a thirty-two mile march to Kangma in one day was not an inviting undertaking.

Business of the utmost importance was now going on between the Government of India and Colonel Younghusband, and too much delay was taking place in the transmission of telegrams, which had to be carried a long way by Mounted Infantry. On June 5, therefore, Colonel Younghusband decided to proceed forthwith to Chumbi so as to be at the telegraph office and reply to important despatches directly they arrived. Orders were issued that evening that Colonel Younghusband would leave Gyantse at 3 A.M. next day escorted by forty-five Mounted Infantry under the command of Major Murray, 8th Gurkhas, my blood-poisoned arm keeping me still in the post. It was hard luck, as it was the second time the company and I were separated owing to misfortune.

Colonel Younghusband went through to Kangma that day, where they halted for the night, and were to go on next morning to Kalatso. There was not sufficient room in the post to admit of the extra Mounted Infantry being put inside, and they were therefore picketed outside in the open, together with the Yak Corps, under Lieutenant Wigram, and their escort of about twenty men of the 1st Battalion 2nd Gurkhas. About 4 A.M. next day the Mounted Infantry saddled up and were waiting to start with Colonel Younghusband for Kalatso; most of the men, at the invitation of their comrades, the two companies of the 23rd Sikh Pioneers garrisoning Kangma, were inside the post having some warm tea, and Subadar Sangat Singh and Jemadar Prem Singh and about six or eight men were with the ponies. Most of the yaks and over half the Gurkha escort were well on their way to Kalatso, and the rest were just ready to go, when Jemadar Prem Singh, of the Mounted Infantry, who had walked about 200 yards up the hill, espied about 1,000 Tibetans get up out of a nullah where they had concealed themselves, and make straight for the post. The Jemadar ran back and gave the alarm, and Subadar Sangat Singh, thinking of his ponies, collected the five or six Sikh and Gurkha Mounted Infantry men, who, lying down practically in the open, prepared to defend their ponies, and well they did it, else the lot would have been either killed, wounded, or cut loose. The few Gurkhas with the yaks, who were still further in front and nearest the enemy, did splendidly and fell back fighting on to the Subadar, all except one man, who spurned retirement, and facing hundreds of Tibetans alone, died a soldier's death, a credit to himself, and an example for the whole of the Indian army. The attack was so sudden that although the Subadar and his party shot down numbers of the enemy and checked them, some had got in amongst the ponies and were killing them, cutting them loose, or trying to ride them away. Some Tibetans had even mounted, without loosing the picketing rope, but were unused to the slippery English saddles, and the ponies, resenting this rude treatment, bucked them off again. Just then the Mounted Infantry men inside the post, hearing the commotion outside, rushed out with fixed bayonets and drove the Tibetans out of the pony lines, untied the ponies and took them all inside the post, still covered by the Subadar and his party.

Captain Pearson and his garrison of two companies of the 23rd had commenced magazine fire on the Tibetans, and soon they were compelled to retire, leaving numbers of dead behind. Colonel Younghusband and Lieutenant Franklin, who had also come from Gyantse, plied their rifles well and accurately, as did Major Murray, who, although the senior officer present, with the utmost courtesy would not interfere with Captain Pearson in the defence of his own post. Immediately the Tibetans showed signs of going, Captain Pearson sallied out of the post with one company of the 23rd, led by their fine old Subadar, Jiwan Singh, an old Afghan War and Roberts's march veteran. Moreover, the Mounted Infantry, turning out sharp, caused the wavering Tibetans to turn and fly. They did not know that so large a body of Mounted Infantry was in the post, and had tarried just too long; they were caught by the mounted men, who, led by their own native officers, rode through them, using their rifles from horseback, and chased them down the Gyantse road, and up the Ralung road. The attack had completely failed, and the Tibetans had sense enough never to attempt another on posts in the lines of communication, which, though weakly held, were proved to the Tibetans to be capable of withstanding their assaults. Our losses at Kangma were trivial, and were one man of the Gurkha yak escort and one follower killed, and three men of the 23rd wounded. The

1st Mounted Infantry had three men wounded, three ponies killed, and three ponies lost. Major Murray and Lieutenant Franklin lost both their ponies, which had been cut loose by the Tibetans.

About 9 A.M. Colonel Younghusband continued his journey to Chumbi, escorted by the 1st Mounted Infantry for eight miles, where an escort of the 2nd Mounted Infantry was ready to take him on. On the road they met Major Lye with a company of the 23rd coming along in all haste to help at Kangma. He had heard of the attack from the flying yak-drivers, who had done the twelve miles between the posts in record time, and promptly turned out, and was marching to the relief till met by Colonel Younghusband, who explained the situation.

The Mounted Infantry not having returned on the day they were expected caused some anxiety at Gyantse, and we were all glad to see them turning up very pleased with themselves on the afternoon of the 8th. My arm had nearly recovered, and being wearied of staying in the post I went out with the remaining twenty Mounted Infantry to reconnoitre up the Lhasa road, replenish the commissariat, get information about the enemy, and find out what had happened to the Mounted Infantry who had gone to Kangma. The few Tibetans we met told us wonderful yarns about thousands of the enemy being collected in the vicinity, and, strange to say, none of them knew anything about the attack on Kangma. We returned to the post with one pony, 350 sheep and goats, and in a few minutes the stalwart mountain gunners were busy hunting through the sheep and goats to find any milch ones, as it was a long time since they had had any fresh milk. In addition five prisoners were brought in to be questioned on the whereabouts and numbers of the enemy. It may be remarked that it was a most unpleasant duty questioning the Tibetan peasants met with in the fields, as the interview was bound to be observed by some Tibetan soldiers, Lama, or spy, and it was well known to us that the unfortunate peasant, either man or woman, who was seen talking to us, would be the recipient of Tibetan vengeance. It was preferable therefore to bring them into the post as prisoners and there question them, so that they had the appearance of submitting to compulsion.

About 1 A.M. on the 10th the Tibetans in large numbers made another night attack on the post, their main body holding all the partially destroyed villages all round, and illuminating the darkness of the night by the flashes from the discharges of their guns and rifles. Their sharpshooters, armed with modern rifles, chiefly express, came closer in, some taking up their positions on the parapet of the bridge over the Gyantse River, within 120 yards of the Mounted Infantry breastwork, and kept up a sustained fire for about three hours on the post. The night being dark, it missed us, and hit the tops of the houses in the post, which showed up better. This demonstration was accompanied by fire from all the jingals in the jong, quite the best-directed yet experienced. Their bullets came over the post and crashed into the wooden *parados* behind the Mounted Infantry breastwork which had been constructed by the Royal Engineers, and that night their work was thoroughly appreciated, as, but for the *parados*, the men lining the breastwork must have had heavy casualties. About 3 A.M. the enemy drew off from the post and concentrated their attentions, first on the Gurkha Post and then on Palla. Having surrounded the Gurkha Post in a shouting frenzied mob, they began to taunt the Gurkhas, and we were treated to quite an interesting conversation between the two parties. The Tibetans commenced by saying that the Gurkhas were terrible cowards in not coming out of their post and fighting them in the open. The Gurkha Jemadar replied that they were horrid cowards in not coming on and attacking them, as he had only twenty men, while they had thousands. After this came dead silence for a few minutes, and then the Tibetans, making a hideous row, rushed up to within twenty yards of the Gurkha Post, exposing themselves freely. Now was the Gurkha Jemadar's chance, and he made the best of it, as he opened the most perfectly controlled magazine fire on them, which, rattling out in the stillness of the night, sounded like 5,000 rifles, although he had only got fifty. Above all we could hear his whistle sound, and immediately the firing ceased, and again his word of command 'Continue,' when the fifty rifles rang out again. It was too much for the Tibetans, and they stopped their jackal cries and slunk off leaving six of their number dead behind them. It seemed that all was over for that night, when a terrific shindy was heard from the direction of Palla village, followed by a loud explosion, and then by a roar of magazine fire from the garrison of 32nd Pioneers. The Tibetans had the impertinence to attempt to blow up the Pioneers in Palla with gunpowder. Again there was silence, which continued, and which we were all glad of, as it was about 4 A.M. and everybody was terribly sleepy and cold; so after the usual potion of several cups of hot cocoa, always to be found ready on these occasions in the 32nd Pioneer mess, we went to bed again.

Only one Tibetan was killed at Palla that night. Both the Gurkha Jemadar and the Sikh Subadar were very disgusted at the small losses they had inflicted on the Tibetans. The Gurkha Jemadar said, in a tone of superiority, that all his men were recruits, and got nervous and did not depress their rifles sufficiently to hit the enemy; while the

Sikh Subadar, with his solemn, thoughtful face, said that it was the 'beiman ki kismat' (that it was the good fortune of the unfaithful ones), and that although he had fired 385 of the best gollies (bullets) in the world, only one of the Tibetans got in their way and was hit.

They both forgot, or would not admit, the difficulties and general fruitlessness of rifle-fire at night. From this time on the Mounted Infantry were more busily engaged than ever, as it was necessary to lay in a stock of provisions and fodder, particularly the latter, for General Macdonald's force, which was now about to march from Chumbi.

All the grain and fodder in the adjacent villages had either been sold to us previous to the commencement of hostilities, or had been removed before the destruction of those villages. It was, therefore, necessary to go further afield, and it fell to the lot of the Mounted Infantry to find daily fodder and grain. About forty or fifty Mounted Infantry and one hundred mules escorted by fifty infantry used to go out daily, and when the Mounted Infantry found the stuff, the mules and escort came along and carried it in; while the Mounted Infantry scoured the hills to find sheep, goats, and cattle. These expeditions used generally to be productive of a little excitement, as the Tibetans would sometimes show themselves with the intention of cutting us off; but a few men advanced in their direction and a few shots were sufficient to send them flying, as at this time they had a wholesome respect for Mounted Infantry, and would not engage them in the open. Other days we would get very good shooting—gazelle, hares, snow-cock, and partridges—the best day producing, six gazelle, two snow-cock, eight hares, and a partridge, all being most welcome in the messes, where everybody was tired of Tibetan mutton served up in various forms at every meal.

Then always the Mounted Infantry, bringing in their booty, used to run the gauntlet of the Tibetan fire, as they passed through the wood.

On the 11th we went down the river towards the Tsechen monastery to see how the enemy were getting on there, and also to find out if the stone bridge over the river just below the monastery was held on either or both banks. We got past the monastery and on to the bridge before the Tibetans knew we had arrived, and found that this end of the bridge was only covered by fire from Tsechen, and that the other end was protected by a small fortified village about 200 yards from the bridge-head. From both these places the Tibetans now opened fire; but they were too late, and having found out what was required, the men, well extended, galloped clear of their fire, and escaped with only one pony slightly wounded. There was a small house about 500 yards north-west of the Gurkha Post, and about 500 yards from the jong. On the morning of the 12th it was discovered that the Tibetans had, during the night, built a covered way from the jong to this house, copying the many covered ways Captain Shepherd with his men and the Tibetan prisoners had dug connecting the Gurkha Post, Palla, and other places with the post. They had loopholed the whole of this covered way, and had mounted two small cannon in it, which fired through port-holes with stone blinds, thus bringing a flanking fire to bear on the Gurkha Post and the post. Lieutenant Hadow and a Maxim went to the Gurkha Post, and tried to enfilade the work, and so a duel went on for the rest of the day. Next night the Gurkha Jemadar and twenty of his men crept softly up to the house, and found twelve armed Tibetans fast asleep. The Gurkhas, wishing to make them prisoners, tied their pigtails together; but during this operation the Tibetans woke up, and, in spite of the Gurkhas telling them that nothing would happen to them if they did not make a noise, yet they shouted out and tried to escape, waking up all their comrades sleeping behind the covered way. So, after firing a volley down the covered way, the Gurkhas retired, while the Tibetans in the jong, thinking that there was no doubt about their being attacked, treated us to another display of fireworks from the jong, which they kept up for about an hour. The plucky little Gurkha Jemadar had planned and carried out this surprise entirely on his own initiative, and with marked success, as the Tibetans never went into that house again.

The Mounted Infantry had spent the day collecting grain and fodder, and had made a very good haul. On the 13th Lieutenant Gurdon, with twenty Mounted Infantry and eighty Pioneers, with all the transport available, went to Kangma for ammunition and stores. That night the Tibetans again surrounded the Gurkha Post and Palla village, and in the morning the respective native officers signalled in their doings. The Gurkha Post reported four, and Palla three, of the enemy as killed.

The following day Captain Shepherd, with a strong working party, went down the left bank of the river to level to the ground the already partially destroyed villages. Major Murray commanded two companies of Gurkhas and the Mounted Infantry, and two ten-pounder guns, as covering party. We went about two miles down the river, and put out a line of Mounted Infantry piquets. Large crowds of Tibetans, both mounted and on foot, came out of the jong and monastery, skirmishing about on the right bank of the river, which they eventually crossed by the stone bridge near Tsechen monastery, and tried to get round us. Just then a signalled message from the post told us to look sharp, for 400 mounted men and 600 footmen were trying to work round us. The guns opened on them with shrapnel at 4,000 yards; but the ground affording such good cover, we who were closer could see that the Tibetans were not suffering. All this time they were firing away at us from about 1,000 yards, and we were quite surprised at hearing so many modern rifle bullets singing over our heads, showing that they were not badly armed. They never got close, for whenever they showed up, the Mounted Infantry piquets let them have it so hot that they thought discretion the better part of valour. When Captain Shepherd had finished his work after about four hours, he went back to the post, and Major Murray sent a message saying that he would make a pretence of retiring, but would lie up under cover and try to draw the Tibetans on. We retired by alternate sections, and kept ten men about 200 yards behind. This made the Tibetans follow up well; but they still maintained a very civil distance. Finally they stopped about two miles from the post, and would not be drawn any nearer. They then commenced burning any villages and fodder they came across, so that we should not get the latter.

The mail escort, on the way back from Kangma, passing through a narrow place on the road, was fired on by Tibetans 100 yards off, and only escaped because the Havildar in charge, having previously extended his men twenty yards apart, galloped through the defile, and so got through with only one pony slightly wounded. The Tibetans, having delivered their fire, bolted headlong into some caves high up in the rocky sides of the valley, where they took cover from the sharp fire directed on them by the Havildar and his party.

The convoy was expected back on the 16th, and information was received that a body of Tibetans was waiting to attack it, at the same place where they had fired on the post escort. Captain Cullen, with 100 of the 32nd and the whole of the Mounted Infantry, went to meet the convoy, starting from Gyantse at 4 A.M. The Mounted Infantry went ahead quickly, and joined the convoy just as it was leaving its night's camp. The post was sent on with twelve men, and we returned with the convoy. Whether on account of the timely assistance from Gyantse, or wrong information about the Tibetan movements, it is difficult to say, but the Tibetans did not even appear until the convoy had passed well out on the Gyantse plain, where there was little chance of molesting it. The Mounted Infantry were rear-guard, and had halted at the confluence of the two streams on the plain, when a lot of Tibetans were seen moving about in a copse near the river. At first they were thought to be unarmed, and nothing was done to them, but the moment we moved off towards Gyantse, they, thinking we were gone for good, left the copse and commenced running across to some good cover near the road by which the post escort would return. It was now evident that they were armed, and that they were going to waylay the post escort again. The Mounted Infantry rounded on them, and taking them in rear, made them bolt for their lives up into the hills. Four of them were killed, and, the returning post escort having arrived, we returned to Gyantse without further incident, except the usual daily fire from the jong, which was always greater the day a convoy came in. This day's work was most beneficial, as the Tibetans never again attempted to attack the post escort on its outward or inward journey.

The convoy contained a commodity which was to alter all the features of fighting in Tibet, and was to save the small force from what must otherwise have been very heavy losses, and therefore the necessity of further reinforcements from India. This was the common shell for the ten-pounder guns of the British Mountain Battery, the ammunition of which had hitherto been shrapnel and case-shot, both being equally useless against Tibetan massively built jongs, or even sangars. This having been ascertained, fifty rounds per gun were hastily made up at the Cossaipore Arsenal, and sent up. Captain Easton, commanding the section of the battery, beamed with satisfaction when he saw his new shells, and all were pleased that at last we had a match for the Tibetan 'William,' 'Billy,' and 'Little Billies,' as their guns had been named. The following day, the 17th, was fixed for their first experiment on the jong, which had been made impervious to rifle bullets, and the Tibetans believed that our artillery was equally powerless to harm them. We were not to see the shell practice, as we had to go foraging; but we saw the effects on the large masonry building in the jong on our way back to the post in the evening. The guns with unerring aim had planted seven shells in the same spot on this wall, which was about four feet thick, making a breach about four feet square, which the Tibetans were now busy building up again. That morning a patrol of the 32nd from Palla house had quite a fight of their own. They were attacked by about fifty Tibetans who tried to ambuscade them—an attempt for which they paid dearly, as twenty-one of them were killed.

Milk and meat were again getting short at the post, but the deficiency was remedied on the 18th, the Mounted Infantry having had a lucky day foraging. They got 100 mule-loads of boosa (fodder), eight cows, and 1,181 sheep and goats, so that the gunners and the Norfolk Maxim men, and in fact every spare man in the post, were milking away as hard as they could up to dark. This was the day on which, as already recorded, I made my best bag of both fur and feathers, to the great relief of our monotonous *cuisine*.

We heard from the natives in the hills, in the Khamba Jong direction, that 1,000 Tibetan soldiers were marching through the hills direct from Shigatse to Niru on the cross-road from the Karo Là to Kangma, east of our lines of communication, of whom more will be related. The Tibetans attempted to blow up the Gurkha piquet-house that morning, and the stolid little Gurkhas slew eight of them and dispersed the rest.

The following day we got more boosa, and again on the 19th and 21st. Information having been gathered that large bodies of Tibetans, besides the 8,000 or 10,000 in the jong, were blocking all the roads about twelve to twenty miles out, Colonel Brander considered it safer to send the post to Kangma only when it was absolutely necessary to correspond with the General, and on those occasions to send a full section of Mounted Infantry under a native officer as escort. These would go to Kangma one day, stay the night, and return the following day—sixty-four miles in two consecutive days. The post of the 21st brought the news that the

General and his force would arrive at Kangma on the 23rd, and Gyantse on the 25th.

Efforts to bring in fodder had, therefore, to be redoubled as we knew the General's force would be much in need of it. On the night of the 23rd the Tibetans made a very determined attack on Palla village, supported by a vigorous cannonade from the jong.

A message was lamped to the native officer in command that star-shell would be fired from the post, and that they must reserve their fire till the enemy were shown up by it. The star-shell from Bubble and Squeak were, alas! a failure, only one out of several igniting properly, they having been too long in stock. The Tibetans were amazed at this new kind of devilry, and stopped firing for a bit; but when they found that the star-shell did no harm, they burst forth into peals of catcalls, and renewed their firing. However, the native officer had got in a few useful volleys, which made the attackers on Palla draw off.

Next evening a star-shell practice took place with little better result. At every shell that was fired, 'William' slung his 4½-pound bullet into the post, making the star-shell experimentalists duck under cover. During the day we had been foraging, and were searching an empty monastery about four miles up the Lhasa road. Neither grain nor fodder was to be found, the Tibetans having removed all that had been left on our last visit to their camp at Gubshi. Nearly all these men were out of the monastery preparatory to returning to the post, and the last two or three men were coming along very leisurely, thinking that, the place having been searched, there was no enemy in it. There were some all the same, concealed in an underground cellar, and one of them fired at the men through an invisible hole. The bullet passed between the legs of two of the men, making them skip in a way which I am sure they never did before in their lives. Luckily they were not hit. A further search was immediately made, but no cellar or hole could be found, and as the concealed warrior did not fire another shot, the honours of the incident were certainly with him.

That night was again made hideous by another attack on Palla. The enemy put several bags of powder into an empty house near Palla; this they exploded with great *éclat* and cheering, but took good care to keep clear of the Pioneer Post.

On the 24th Lieutenant Coleridge took all the transport animals to Kangma, escorted by a hundred Gurkhas and twenty-two Mounted Infantry. The Tibetans gave him a lively time of it on the road above Naini, but he fortunately escaped with one or two mules hit.

At 1 A.M. the Tibetans made another onslaught on Palla. It was most annoying to the whole of the Gyantse garrison to be wakened up and turned out every night like this. The only person who improved on it was the mess-servant of the 32nd Pioneers, who at the first shot would get up and make hot cocoa and coffee.

Not having had any news of the General and his force, on the 25th Colonel Brander sent out the Mounted Infantry to ascertain what was going on. When we got near Naini monastery, there were sounds of firing, but as the place had been reconnoitred the day before and found unoccupied it was thought that the firing could not be from there. However, we soon discovered that it was, and that the defences had been improved and were strongly held. Anxious to find out whom the Tibetans were firing at, we continued until we came upon Captain Peterson, of the 2nd Mounted Infantry, with half his company, having a brush with the enemy. He said that the force had camped that day at Lantang, and would reach Gyantse next day. While we were talking, one of his men received a severe wound, of which he died in a few days. When hit, he was about 350 yards from the monastery wall, on open ground, from which it was very difficult to get him away without more loss; but a plucky Afridi, at great personal risk, and on his own initiative, rushed in, picked him up, and brought him away safely.

CHAPTER IX

RELIEVING FORCE ARRIVES—THE CAPTURE OF TSECHEN AND GYANTSE JONG

THE reason why General Macdonald and his column did not reach Gyantse was now disclosed. When his first column reached Kangma on the 22nd, a reconnoitring party of the 2nd Mounted Infantry, having proceeded up the Kangma-Ralung road (which will be remembered as cutting off the right-hand corner of the Y formed by the meeting of the roads at Gyantse), found a large force of Tibetans in position at Niru, estimated at 800 to 1,000 men. This was the same body of the enemy that we had heard of on the 18th as passing through the hills in the Khamba Jong direction. Its object in holding that road was to prevent the General's force from proceeding that way to the Karo Là and Lhasa, which, of course, he had no intention of doing. On the 23rd a column of 500 men, two guns, and fifty of the 1st and 2nd Mounted Infantry (twenty-one of the 1st Mounted Infantry garrisoning Kangma), all under Colonel Hogge, marched against the Tibetans at Niru.

They, however, did not wait to be turned out, but decamped early that morning, not thinking their wall high enough to stop a British force. About half of them joined another force holding Gubshi, and the rest came into Gyantse Jong, where they were not well received by their own generals, and were ordered out on the night of the 24th–25th to hold Naini monastery.

Colonel Hogge rejoined the General's column on the 24th, and the march to Gyantse was resumed on the 25th, and this accounts for the delay in arriving. When we returned to Gyantse on the evening of the 25th, and reported to Colonel Brander the state of affairs, he decided to take out his flying column and co-operate with the General in the capture of Naini next day. He started early next morning, and took his four guns and infantry up the enormous heights overlooking Naini from the Gyantse side, and sent the 1st Mounted Infantry up the ordinary road to block that line of escape. The General's force arriving from the other direction at 9 A.M., the 900 Tibetans were hemmed in on all sides in Naini. The action was opened by Captain Peterson, commanding the advanced guard, composed of the 2nd Mounted Infantry, twenty-one of the 1st, and fifty of the 40th Pathans. They all went at it with a will, and cleared the Tibetans out of several of the outlying houses; but it was soon seen that the thirty-foot wall of Naini monastery required some shelling and guncotton before they could get in. They also found that the village between Naini and the river was strongly held. A company of the 23rd and a company of the 32nd cleared the village, all except one house, which was so strongly barricaded that, although the men of the 23rd were endeavouring to make a hole in the wall with their bayonets, without guncotton they could not get in, and had to retire to give the artillery an opportunity of battering it. Here the 23rd lost two men killed and two wounded, and Lieutenant Turnbull, of that regiment, greatly distinguished himself in carrying a wounded man to a place of safety. The Tibetans in this house behaved splendidly, and although battered with seven-pounder shells from 250 yards, did not cease fire till the guns had knocked down most of the front face of the house. They lay low in the house till late in the evening, but could not resist firing at the rear guard as it was passing, killing one of the Gurkhas. The rear guard immediately stormed the house and burnt part of it; but when they had marched on about 500 yards, the original Tibetans in the house came to life again and fired away as well as ever. Meanwhile, Colonel Brander's guns from the heights, and the other four guns of No. 7 Mountain Battery which had arrived with the General, shelled the monastery, and taking the Tibetans in reverse drove them from their loopholes. The 40th Pathans, having worked up to the back wall, found a ladder in position by which they made their entry. The Mounted Infantry, the 23rd, and 32nd broke in the main gate, and then the hardest of the fighting began. The Tibetans had taken refuge in the houses and cellars, and were, as usual in those places, fighting well. Major Lye, of the 23rd, leading his men into a house thronged with Tibetans, was cut down by them, and very severely wounded on the head and left hand, and was well saved by his own men. Several houses and cellars were blown in with guncotton, and the occupants killed or captured, and now, as the whole place was occupied, the General, not wishing to punish them any further, ordered the march to Gyantse to be continued at 3 P.M.

The Tibetans lost about 150 in killed, wounded, and prisoners, and must have been thankful that the whole 900 of them were not despatched.

Our losses were five men killed, Major Lye, a native officer of the 2nd Mounted Infantry, and nine men all badly wounded. Amongst the wounded was one man of the 1st Mounted Infantry who had come from Kangma. The rest of the 1st Mounted Infantry spent the day waiting for the chance that never came, the Tibetans thinking it safer to remain in the monastery than to try conclusions again in the open.

The relieving force were inclined to scoff at the stories of the jingals in the jong, but they changed their minds when, crossing the Gyantse stream at the end of the wood, they found the jingal bullets clattering about them, although they were 2,000 yards away. A British gunner who had his helmet knocked to pieces by one of them expressed his disapprobation in very strong language. An officer of experience, paying a courteous visit to old friends in the post, confessed he never did so much bullet-dodging in his life as in those last 500 yards through the wood into the post.

The General's force looked like a big army to those who had been at Gyantse, but numbered only about 2,000 rifles and eight guns, a wee force to capture the capital of a hostile country.

It comprised the remaining four guns of No. 7 British Mountain Battery, four guns of the 30th Native Mountain Battery, four companies Royal Fusiliers, four companies 23rd Sikh Pioneers, four companies 8th Gurkhas, four companies 32nd Sikh Pioneers, eight companies 40th Pathans, the 2nd Mounted Infantry, twenty-one men of the 1st, and one section of the 3rd Mounted Infantry, hospitals, ordnance, &c., and over 3,000 transport animals. It was the latter which made the column look so big.

The 27th was a nasty wet day, and the troops were given a halt. A column was detailed for next day to go down the left bank of the river (*i.e.* in the Shigatse direction), and drive the enemy out of all the villages as far as Tsechen monastery, and if time allowed to storm that monastery and jong.

Colonel Brander, with the 32nd, was to start at 3 A.M. on the 28th, and go down the right bank of the river, and occupy two small villages near the river, so as to prevent the Tibetans in the jong from sending reinforcements to Tsechen.

It rained hard all night, and up to 11 A.M. on the 28th. 8 A.M. had been fixed for the column to move off; but owing to the wet, the Royal Fusiliers had been unable to cook during the night, and to give them a chance of getting some food the advance of the column was postponed for two hours.

Much to the satisfaction of the 1st Mounted Infantry, old scores with Tsechen were to be wiped out that day. The enemy in Tsechen were not friends of ours, and the company were very pleased to be in the advanced guard of the column going against them. Also it was the first occasion since March and the first action in which the whole company were together. The Royal Fusiliers and 23rd Pioneers were in the first line, the 8th Gurkhas, 40th Pathans, guns, and Maxims in the second.

We found the villages all empty, and saw about 200 horse and foot of the enemy come out from

Tsechen and occupy a village about 1,000 yards in advance. As the column came on, the Mounted Infantry advance guard was sufficient for this party of the enemy, and drove them out of the village they had just occupied, capturing four of their ponies. Near the foot of the Tsechen Hill is a large substantial village in a grove of trees called Gubshi. This used to be occupied by about 500 or 600 Tibetans; but to-day there seemed to be nobody. However, before we could find out, the guns from about 4,000 yards off began to drop shells into it with the utmost accuracy. This settled the question, and there was no enemy within when the first line got up to it. The Mounted Infantry orders were to become the left flank guard when nearing Gubshi, and moving out to take up their position they saw a lot of Tibetans escaping up into the hills on the left, so gave chase, scattering them and capturing six more ponies. The rest of the mounted Tibetans did not stop till they got to Dongtse, twelve miles down the Shigatse road.

A short description of Tsechen Hill and position is necessary. It is another of those hills that stand by themselves on the plain. This one in shape resembles the side view of a great whale lying on a flat surface, tail to the left, head to the right. It is about one mile long, and the highest point about 600 feet above the plain, and very

TSE CHEN.

narrow. Near the right end, or head, the monastery and village are built. The monastery extends up the face of the hill from the plain to the summit of the ridge, and is surrounded by a ten-foot wall nearly all the way. The jong is built on the highest point of the ridge about midway between both ends. From the jong towards the left the ridge slopes down to the plain in a system of sharp and jagged boulders. Both the front face and the back face are practically inaccessible, and impossible for troops to get up under fire, except at the monastery itself. The jong was a massive stone loopholed building, and the houses in the monastery of the same class. Gubshi village, near the left end of the hill, was expected to have been strongly held, but it proved to be otherwise, and therefore, as it was still early in the day, the General issued his orders for the assault of the monastery and jong. Four companies of the 40th Pathans were sent against the village and the monastery, and two companies of the 8th Gurkhas, commencing on the extreme left, scrambled up the tortuous path through the rocks and boulders towards the jong. All the guns, Maxims, and rifles of the reserves covered these movements by a concentrated fire on the jong and monastery.

The 40th advanced across the open plain with all the *élan* of the Pathan, and dashed into the monastery just as the Gurkhas from amongst the rocks opened fire on the jong at 200 yards range. The ten-pounder common shells had breached the jong splendidly, and the gunners kept up their fire till the Gurkhas were within eighty yards of it, so that the enemy could not stand to their loopholes to fire on the Gurkhas. The co-operation between the guns and infantry was beautiful, and crowned with success. The Tibetans could not stand it, and took to their heels before the Gurkhas got to the jong; at any rate, few remained to oppose them, and these they soon disposed of. More or less the same took place in the monastery, and most of the enemy bolted over the ridge or hid in the cellars as soon as the 40th gained the lowest houses. One large house at the top held out until the gate was blown in by Captain Shepherd and his sappers.

Almost the whole place was in the hands of the 40th when Captain Craster, of that regiment, was shot dead. His day's work was finished, and done well, and it was a sad fatality that claimed him at its close.

The orders for the Mounted Infantry were to wait under cover near the left end of the hill, and to allow the enemy to get well out on the plain before pursuing them. They halted behind a convenient chorten, or Tibetan monumental wall, whence a good view of the plain behind the Tsechen Hill was obtained, and where they were well concealed. They and two companies of the 23rd Pioneers, in Gubshi village, were told off as the left flank guard, and I was directed to take charge of the whole. Lieutenant Bailey had rejoined the 1st Mounted Infantry since the arrival of the General's force. He was instructed to pursue when he saw a good opportunity, and to send word when he went off, so that if possible I should follow him. Behind the Tsechen Hill, along the bank of the river, is a patch of scrub-jungle about three miles long and a mile broad. The Tibetans, having been ejected by the Pathans and Gurkhas, were soon seen dropping from the rear walls of the jong and monastery in large numbers, and plunging down the rear face of the hill, and making for the jungle. The Mounted Infantry now pursued, and swept through the jungle in line, playing havoc with the enemy. Lieutenant Bailey having sent an orderly to me before starting, and the two companies of the 23rd having been ordered to join their regiment, I followed the Mounted Infantry and met them returning from their pursuit. They had been right through the piece of jungle, and pressed the Tibetans so hard that many of them jumped into the river.

Now, if there is anything in the world a Tibetan hates it is water, so that they must have been *in extremis* when they tried to cross a river. They found this of no avail either, as one section of the

Mounted Infantry plunged in, and with their ponies swam across. Most of the Tibetans were drowned. There was a small village on the other side of the river, and the section of Mounted Infantry, seeing some mounted Tibetans going into it, charged into it also, and captured ten ponies and six prisoners.

While we were waiting for the company to reassemble large numbers of Tibetans were seen escaping from the jong and monastery, and coming down the hill, some hiding amongst the rocks and caves, and others going into a small village at the base of the hill. These, of course, had to be turned out. The Mounted Infantry on their way came into sight on the right side of Tsechen Hill, where they were not expected, and, being a long distance off, were mistaken for the enemy by an excited Maxim, which greeted us with a few rounds before recognising us. Lieutenant Bailey, with about thirty men, went for the village, and the remainder, dismounting, attacked up the almost precipitous rear face of the hill towards the jong and monastery. The rocks and caves were swarming with Tibetans, and all the men were soon engaged individually. Those of the enemy who laid down their arms were taken prisoners both here and in the village. Before ascending the hill a shot was fired from the point of the hill where the jingal that commanded the bridge used to be. Two Gurkhas begged permission to go and slay the firer with their kukeries. This being granted, off they went in great glee, but the Tibetan was too nimble for them and got away.

When the Mounted Infantry commenced their pursuit the guns were firing at the jong and monastery, and any shells that went over their mark came screaming above the company. One common shell was seen to strike the ground and explode quite three miles beyond the Tsechen Hill; others either did not explode or fell into the jungle, where the explosion would have escaped notice. Three shrapnel burst over the company, and probably owing to their being 800 or 900 feet up at the time of burst, or to the wide extension of the Mounted Infantry, no damage was done. These shells afforded a good experience for the men and excellent training.

It was raining hard and quite dark when we fell in to march to camp. The plain had become a marsh, and many were the falls that took place before the men and ponies were settled down in their lines in their new camp, as during the day the camp had been shifted to the left bank, and a mile below the post, to make the Tibetans in Gyantse Jong think that the attack would come from the Shigatse direction.

This day's work was a terrible shock to the

Tibetans in Gyantse Jong, as they had placed great reliance in the immense strength of Tsechen and Naini monasteries and their respective garrisons of 1,000 and 900 men. That night a leakage of Tibetans commenced from Gyantse Jong, and by July 6 the garrison of 8,000 or 10,000 men had dwindled down to about 4,000 or 5,000.

Considering the number of good rifles and ammunition captured at Tsechen, and the strength of the garrison and place itself, our losses were ridiculously small. Captain Craster, of the 40th, was killed, Captains Bliss and Humphreys, of the 8th, wounded (slight), and seven rank-and-file wounded.

Early in the morning of the 29th the 1st Mounted Infantry and one company of the 40th were sent to visit and occupy Tsechen, and the jong was blown up by Lieutenant Walker, Captain Shepherd's understudy in the explosive art.

Thirty men of the 1st Mounted Infantry, under Lieutenant Bailey, and the company of the 40th were left as a garrison till the 7th.

Major Bretherton, with his foraging parties, had now a new field of action open to him, as the plain behind Tsechen Hill in the Shigatse direction was rich in grain and boosa, and had not previously been touched.

The Tibetans now began to talk of wishing to meet Colonel Younghusband in Durbar, who immediately granted them an armistice till twelve noon next day, the 30th. Early next morning another flag of truce came in to beg for an extension, saying that the Ta Lama, who was to represent the Tibet Council of State, being old and decrepit, could not travel from Shigatse to Gyantse in one day, and therefore would be unable to arrive before the morning of the 1st. Colonel Younghusband agreed, and extended the armistice till twelve noon on the 1st. It was afterwards ascertained that the Ta Lama had been at Dongtse, twelve miles off, where he was carrying out his duties of Quartermaster-General to the Tibetan army, and that he could easily have come to the Durbar on the 30th, but, being proud and obstinate, and to show his own people that he could make the British Commissioner wait his convenience, he condescended to tell a lie.

The old gentleman arrived at Gyantse on the 1st, but sent in a message that he could not meet Colonel Younghusband till he had conferred with other Tibetan diplomats who had come from Lhasa, and with the Tongsa Pendlop of Butan, who had been appointed by the Dalai Lama as mediator between him and the British. Colonel Younghusband again agreed, and the Durbar was fixed for twelve noon on the 2nd.

This time the Ta Lama did keep his appointment, and turned up accompanied by the Tongsa

Pendlop of Butan and the Lord High Chamberlain to the Dalai Lama, a truculent, ill-looking gentleman, who suffered from a chronic pain in his stomach, which was visibly intensified when the proceedings of the Durbar took a turn other than he wished.

Colonel Younghusband told them that as they had attacked without provocation a peaceful British Mission coming into their country, and kept them in a state of siege for the past two months, before discussing any terms of negotiation they must, to prevent further hostilities, dismiss their troops from Gyantse Jong, the Karo Là and Yung Là[1] Passes, and Dongtse Jong.

These princes of argument gave their reply in an instant, and said they would do so provided Colonel Younghusband would send all his troops back over the Jelap. This preposterous proposal was refused, and they were told that they could have till to-morrow to think it over and give their answer. At this they took their departure, all well pleased except the man with the pain in his stomach, which by his appearance had become much worse.

When the Tongsa Pendlop heard their reply to Colonel Younghusband's proposal, without any pretence at hiding it, he burst out laughing, and

[1] This pass leads N.E. from Gyantse to the valley of the Rong Chu, a tributary of the Brahmaputra.

COLONEL YOUNGHUSBAND AND THE GENERAL TALKING TO THE TONGSA PENDLOP.

told them they had made, under the circumstances, an impossible request.

On the 3rd the Tongsa Pendlop came about one hour before the time fixed for the Durbar. He wore a grey felt squash hat and handsome blue cloth robe of Butan down to the knees, which were bare, while on his feet and legs were a pair of long stockings and patent-leather French shoes. He showed a pair of enormous calves, and altogether looked so much like a handsome, good-tempered Frenchman, even to the well-cared-for imperial on his chin, that he was christened Alphonse amongst the officers.

Colonel Younghusband and his Staff, in full political uniform, General Macdonald and his Staff, and about thirty officers of the force were all assembled at twelve noon in Durbar, and patiently waited for the Tibetan officials till 1 P.M.; but they came not. Colonel Younghusband then dismissed the Durbar. The non-appearance of the Tibetan officials was a breach of courtesy to Colonel Younghusband, and a direct insult to the British Government; yet Colonel Younghusband bore it all with infinite patience, and still gave them a chance of making up their minds. In the evening he sent them a message that he would give them till twelve noon on the 5th to withdraw their troops from the jong, Karo Là, Yung Là, and Dongtse, else General Macdonald would storm the jong.

To this they gave no reply. From the first the Tibetans broke the armistice, one of the terms of which was that no new defences should be built in the jong, nor old ones improved; yet when they found that Lieutenant Hadow's Maxims did not annoy them, they were busy building new walls every day. The 4th was a day of peace, and so was the 5th till 2 P.M. As the morning wore on excitement amongst the whole force increased, and odds about the Tibetans coming in at twelve were given and taken freely. Towards noon the excitement became intense, and was only relieved by the rattle of a Maxim from the post. Lieutenant Hadow and the Norfolk men had been sitting on their guns with their fingers on the buttons of their Maxims, and one minute past twelve they pressed those buttons, the momentary rattle proclaiming to the force that the Tibetans had not come in. The Norfolks were immediately ordered to stop firing, for although the stipulated hour had gone by, it was thought the Tibetans might not know the time, and to make sure the General gave them till 2 P.M. before he ordered the ten-pounders out to shell the jong. Only a few rounds were fired to show them that we were really in earnest; but the Tibetans were unmoved, and opened on the post with their jingals, and thus decided their own fate.

Further to impress the Tibetans with the idea

that the attack on the jong would come from the north-west or Shigatse side, at 3.30 that afternoon General Macdonald ordered out a column of about eight companies, in which each regiment was represented, and the 1st Mounted Infantry, to make a demonstration on the north-west face of the Gyantse monastery. The column crossed the river by a bridge built by the sappers in uncommonly short time.

About 300 or 400 yards from the monastery is a village, and the orders to the 1st Mounted Infantry were to cross the river and find out if the village was occupied or not; then to reconnoitre another monastery about two miles up in the hills, which was reported to be concealing a big force of Tibetans; and finally to become a left flank guard to the demonstrating column, and ward off any flank attack that might be made on them from the hills. The village soon let us know that it was occupied, as fire was opened from there; but the Mounted Infantry scornfully passed by, leaving it to the tender mercies of the column following after, who quickly rushed it, the Tibetans evacuating, and hastily retiring inside the monastery. The column remained in this village till after dark, keeping up a fire on the Tibetans, who were no doubt deceived, and brought most of their forces from other parts of the jong and monastery to the north-west face. Before withdrawing, one of the Gurkhas was severely wounded. The Mounted Infantry proceeded up into the hills to have a look at the next monastery. The ground was very much cut up with nullahs thirty feet deep, with precipitous sides, and impassable. The monastery was found to be massively built, and occupied by the enemy, and also all the hills behind it for miles were manned with Tibetans and jingals. Having found out what was required, the Mounted Infantry withdrew, and took up their position to cover the left flank of the column, and had to stay there under jingal and rifle fire from the monastery until the column retired after dark. The whole force got back to camp about 9.30 P.M. The greater part of the demonstrating column had to march again at midnight, as they were to be in the column which would assault the jong next morning.

The troops told off for the attack on the jong were:

No. 7 British Mountain Battery (six guns, B.L. ten-pounders).

No. 30 Native Mountain Battery (four guns, M.L. seven-pounders).

8th Gurkhas, Bubble and Squeak (two guns, M.L. seven-pounders).

Royal Fusiliers (two companies).

Norfolk Regiment (Maxim-gun detachment).

Royal Irish Rifles (Maxim-gun detachment).

NO. 7 MOUNTAIN BATTERY ON THE MARCH.

1st Sappers and Miners (one company).

23rd Sikh Pioneers (three companies).

32nd Sikh Pioneers (two companies).

8th Gurkha Rifles (two companies).

40th Pathans (three companies).

2nd Mounted Infantry (one company).

Maxim-gun detachments of 23rd and 32nd Sikh Pioneers.

These were divided into three columns, as under:

Right Column	Central Column	Left Column
Commander, Capt. Johnson, Royal Fusiliers.	*Commander*, Capt. Maclachlan, 40th Pathans.	*Commander*, Major Murray, 8th Gurkhas.
Detachment Sappers and Miners.	Detachment Sappers and Miners.	Detachment Sappers and Miners.
1 Coy. Royal Fusiliers.	1 Coy. 40th Pathans.	1 Coy. 8th Gurkhas.
1 Coy. 23rd Sikh Pioneers.	1 Coy. 23rd Pioneers.	1 Coy. 32nd Pioneers.
1 7-pounder gun (Squeak).		
	RESERVES	
1 Coy. Royal Fusiliers.	2 Cos. 40th Pathans.	1 Coy. 8th Gurkhas.
1 Coy. 23rd Pioneers.		1 Coy. 32nd Pioneers.

The remainder of the troops were to remain in camp, and during the day shift camp to the old position on the right bank of the river.

The guns and Maxims were to take up the following positions:

Two seven-pounders, large, 30th Mountain Battery, one small (Bubble), two Maxims 23rd Pioneers on the spur east of Palla, under Captain Luke, R.A.

Four ten-pounders No. 7 Mountain Battery, two Maxims Royal Irish Rifles, near Palla, under Major Fuller, R.G.A.

Two ten-pounders No. 7 Mountain Battery, two seven-pounders 30th Mountain Battery, two Norfolk Maxims, at the Gurkha Post, under Captain Easton, R.G.A.

The Mounted Infantry were to act as follows:

Half 1st Mounted Infantry at Tsechen Monastery were to reconnoitre ten miles down the Shigatse road, staying out till dark.

Half 1st Mounted Infantry to stay in camp; and, as bad luck would have it, I was set down for field officer of the day.

2nd Mounted Infantry to remain in reserve near Palla, under the orders of G.O.C.

Half 3rd Mounted Infantry to reconnoitre fifteen miles up the Lhasa road and stay out till dark.

Lieut.-Colonel Campbell, D.S.O., 40th Pathans, was to command the assaulting columns the first day.

The actual orders for the assault are given in full in Appendix No. I.

It will be acknowledged that the secret of success in all night attacks depends on the explicitness of the attack orders, so as to ensure cohesion between the attacking columns. In this case the assaulting columns had to arrive at the same time at three different points in a village the front of which is quite a mile and a half long. To do so the troops had to march in *détour* a distance of four miles, and it was due to the comprehension by them and the thoroughness of the attack orders that the three assaulting columns did arrive at the same time at the three widely separated points in Gyantse village before the Tibetans were aware of an attack being contemplated or heard the approaching columns.

The command, natural strength, and fortifications of the jong, the large numbers of its defenders, and the voluminous fire delivered by them on many former occasions, gave rise to the general opinion that an assault on the jong would cost our troops at least 250 casualties in killed and wounded. In the dead of night, as the assaulting troops marched out of camp, a feeling of sadness and sympathy for them pervaded those who were left behind. On these occasions it is more trying to be an onlooker than a participator.

As soon as the assault on Gyantse town was delivered it was observed that the enemy's fire was considerably less than on other nights when they thought they were to be attacked. This may be accounted for in two ways. Misled by General Macdonald's demonstration the evening before on the north-west of the monastery, the Tibetans, expecting the real attack to come in the same quarter, withdrew their men, to some extent, from the jong and town in order to strengthen the monastery, and now that the attack came from exactly the opposite direction they were unable to bring their men back in time to resist our attacking columns, and when they tried to do so they were, like Kuropatkin, 'just too late,' and were confined to the monastery and its cover by the gun and rifle fire brought to bear on all parts of the jong, monastery, and town. Again, the leakage caused by the capture of Naini and Tsechen reduced the Tibetan garrison from 8,000 to about 4,000 men, over half of whom were now shut up in the monastery useless.

By 5 A.M. the several columns had gained a footing in the town, and then began a sort of sapping combat. The explosive parties of each column, rushing forward, laid their charges against barricaded houses, and blew in entrances, through which the infantry plunged in and captured the house and its occupants after stubborn hand-to-hand conflict. It was in the leading of one of these explosive parties that Lieutenant Gurdon, of the 32nd, was killed. On three other days had Lieutenant Gurdon been employed in the laying of guncotton charges to houses strongly held by the enemy, all of which were signally successful. Many of the men accompanying him had been killed or wounded, while he escaped unscathed.

He had become so experienced at this dangerous work that nobody expected him to be injured, and the news of his death, therefore, came as a shock to all those who knew him, filling them all with heartfelt sorrow for a gallant soldier and a good friend.

The column under Major Murray had been the most successful and quickest in subduing their portion of the town, and about 9 A.M. the Gurkhas, having passed through the town, charged up to the southern entrance gate of the jong, which was blocked up by a stone sangar, so that an entrance could not be effected. The gallant Gurkhas hung on under cover until they were recalled to the town, as the assault had not yet been properly prepared. At about 11 A.M. the assaulting columns were masters of the assailed portion of the town, and a lull in the day's fighting took place, which was only disturbed by a desultory fire from the jong and casual shots from the guns and Maxims. The midday sun had become very hot, and the troops, after ten hours' marching and fighting, were given a much-needed rest.

About 3.15 P.M. the General signalled the order to the guns to recommence their fire on the jong, and directed Major Fuller to concentrate his ten-pounder gun fire on the south-east wall of the jong between two towers, where he wished the breach to be made. The ten-pounders made perfect shooting and crumbled the wall. The Tibetans responded nobly, and did their best to frustrate by their fire any movement of our troops. About 4 P.M. a powder magazine in the jong was exploded by a well-directed shell, and after this the Tibetan fire decidedly slackened. Colonel Campbell, commanding the assaulting columns, immediately signalled that he was ready to assault, and asked for two companies from the reserve to carry it out. A company of the Royal Fusiliers and a company of the 8th Gurkhas in reserve at Palla village were sent forward, and, led by Colonel Kerr, of the 8th, they dashed across the 800 yards of open ground that separated Palla from the jong. They got across with only two casualties, and assembled in the town, where Colonel Campbell pointed out the place to be assaulted, and launched them on it. The Gurkhas, being more nimble on their feet than the Fusiliers, soon left them behind, and rapidly made their way up the precipitous rocks. The gallant Gurkhas, led by a Scotchman and an Irishman, never checked in their advance up this perilous ascent till they reached the glacis of *débris* caused by the guns in making the breach. Here there was practically no foothold. A Gurkha N.C.O. was seen almost to reach the wall, when he was hit by a stone and fell headlong down at least twenty feet. Numbers of Tibetans had now manned the towers and wall at both sides of the breach, and were hurling down showers of rocks and firing their guns and rifles at the advancing Gurkhas; but nothing could stop the latter, and, stumbling, falling, and scrambling, they reached the breach. Lieutenant Grant[1] was first in, revolver in hand, and shot down several Tibetans. Close on his heels were two or three Gurkhas, then Ireland's representative in Captain Humphreys, adjutant of the 8th Gurkhas, followed by about twenty men. England was not out of it either, as next came, puffing and panting, Lieutenant Franklin, I.M.S., the doctor of the 8th Gurkha Rifles. This officer

[1] THE VICTORIA CROSS.—The *London Gazette* of January 24 announced that the King had signified his intention to confer the decoration of the Victoria Cross upon Lieutenant John Duncan Grant, 8th Gurkha Rifles, for conspicuous bravery in Thibet. The act of courage for which the distinction was conferred was performed upon the occasion of the storming of the Gyantse Jong on the 6th of July last. The storming company, headed by Lieutenant Grant, on emerging from the cover of the village, had to advance up a bare, almost precipitous rock-face, with little or no cover available, and under a heavy fire. Showers of rocks and stones were at the time being hurled down the hillside by the enemy from above. One man could only go up at a time, crawling on hands and knees, to the breach in the curtain. Lieutenant Grant, followed by Havildar Karbir Pun, 8th Gurkha Rifles, at once attempted to scale it, but on reaching near the top he was wounded and hurled back, as was also the Havildar, who fell down the rock some thirty feet. Regardless of their injuries, they again attempted to scale the breach, and, covered by the fire of the men below, were successful in their object, the Havildar shooting one of the enemy on gaining the top. The successful issue of the assault was very greatly due to the splendid example shown by Lieutenant Grant and Havildar Karbir Pun, who has been recommended for the Indian Order of Merit.

had before distinguished himself for pluck and daring at the capture of Palla, and, ever anxious instantly to relieve and aid the first man hit, was now in front of his men cheering them on, or stopping to say a kind word to a wounded man, and giving directions for his removal to a place of safety. The reputation of the Indian Medical Service is high both for pluck and for being where they are most wanted in action, and this officer most certainly raised their proud standard yet higher.

To keep down the Tibetan stone-throwing and firing, and to assist the Gurkhas to get to the breach without terrible loss, General Macdonald ordered Major Fuller to open fire with his ten-pounders on the two towers the moment he saw the Tibetans remanning them. This was nervous work for the gunners, as the towers were 1,000 yards off, and the Gurkhas were within fifty feet of them; yet so perfect was their aim and laying, and so accurate was their gun, that they sent shell after shell into both towers without damaging a single Gurkha.

The jong was now taken, as the Tibetans, seeing the Gurkhas enter *en masse*, did not offer further resistance, but hid themselves in the subterranean passages of that vast rabbit-warren, or escaped by ropes suspended from holes in the wall on the north-west face of the jong. They were lucky in not losing more than about 300 killed and wounded, the number of prisoners being also small. Our troops occupied the jong, and casual shots were fired from the monastery and our side most of the night. Just as the Gurkhas entered the breach a body of Tibetans endeavoured to escape from the jong and monastery towards the hills. Captain Peterson, with the 2nd Mounted Infantry, dashed across the open at them, but before he got near them they returned to the monastery at their best pace.

Early in the day some had also attempted to escape down the Shigatse road, but were stopped by Lieutenant Bailey and his half-company of the 1st Mounted Infantry. The Tibetans, seeing they were hemmed in all round, decided to sit fast in the monastery till well into the night, when the whole body, over 4,000 strong, crept out, and, scattering, made the best of their way to their homes, filled with the steadfast idea that they would never fight the English again.

There was an old tradition amongst the Tibetans that Gyantse Jong was the key to Tibet, and that if it ever fell into the hands of a conqueror further resistance was useless. Notwithstanding the many wars the Tibetans had with the Chinese, Mongolians, Sikhs, Gurkhas, and Butanese, Gyantse Jong had never before been captured. This day's work, therefore, practically put a stop to further fighting in Tibet.

Our losses were more of a surprise than the capture of the jong. They were one British officer and three men killed, seven British officers and three British rank-and-file wounded, one native officer and twenty-two native rank-and-file wounded—total, thirty-seven.

Colonel Campbell, who commanded the assaulting columns, was amongst the wounded. He had a narrow escape, but got off lightly.

Next day the General sent a strong column, under Colonel Hogge, down the Shigatse road to capture Dongtse. With this column were half the 1st Mounted Infantry, under Lieutenant Bailey, and half the 3rd Mounted Infantry, under Major Rowlandson. Dongtse was evacuated, and large quantities of grain and Tibetan stores fell into the hands of the column. The Mounted Infantry went as far as Penam Jong, which was also found empty. This is about thirty miles from Shigatse. On the way the Mounted Infantry came on some of the fugitives, and a few shots having been exchanged they were quickly dispersed. The 1st Mounted Infantry had one pony shot through the neck.

On the same day I was sent off with the other half of the 1st Mounted Infantry to escort 550 mules to Kangma to bring up more stores and ammunition. The whole convoy did the thirty-two miles in seven and a half hours, and got back to Gyantse in two marches, arriving on the 9th.

On the 7th, too, another of those unfortunate gunpowder explosions occurred in the jong, and eight of the Royal Fusiliers sustained terrible injuries, from which three of them died.

The political aspect was not immediately improved by the capture of the jong, as the Tibetan Delegates, including the Ta Lama and the gentleman with the pain in his stomach, had made a record flight over the hills, putting 100 miles between them and the British in twenty-four hours, so that there was nobody left for Colonel Younghusband to confer with. He had therefore no choice left but to advance to Lhasa. General Macdonald, having foreseen this issue, had already made all his arrangements for an advance, so that when asked to do so by Colonel Younghusband he was able to march in a week.

Never was a more popular order issued to a force than that for the advance to Lhasa, especially amongst those who had been in Tibet longest. Its promulgation to the men filled them with delight, and recompensed them for all the cold and hardships they had endured, and all the tsampa (*i.e.* barley-flour) bread they had eaten during the past seven months. There were no more complaints about not getting atta (wheaten flour) for their rations; they were all intent on seeing Lhasa, in the hope, above all other things, that this would secure them a new medal and ribbon, and were willing to eat anything, and to do battle with the whole Tibetan population if necessary.

The weather had now turned very wet and the Gyantse plain had become a quagmire, so the sooner we were away from it the better. The 14th, although pouring with rain, was a gay day for the Mission force, as they did their first march on their way to Lhasa, 150 miles off, another plunge into the unknown. It was known that about ninety miles of the road was through a desolate country where neither food, fodder, nor firewood could be obtained, and the average elevation would be over 15,000 feet. No reliable information was available as to what the Brahmaputra and Lhasa valleys could produce. It was therefore an anxious time for Colonel Younghusband and General Macdonald when they were committed to this unexplored advance. They knew the right time of the year had been selected, and therefore hoped that grazing for the animals would be found. It was impossible to carry fodder for them. Again, it was unknown what force the Tibetans might be able to bring into the field, or the positions, strong or otherwise, they could take up. The Karo Là was known to be almost impregnable if well held, and there might be more positions like it. There were no troops in rear to be drawn upon in case of heavy losses, so the force had to rely on themselves entirely. A force of eight companies, fifty Mounted Infantry (3rd M.I.), and four guns had to be left to hold Gyantse. Other posts had to be garrisoned along the route, which absorbed seventy Mounted Infantry and 400 infantry; so that the force available to march into Lhasa was only 130 Mounted Infantry, eight guns, 1,450 infantry and sappers, and six Maxims, and consisted of:

No. 7 B. M. Battery (6 guns)
No. 30 N. M. Battery (2 guns)
Royal Fusiliers (4 companies)
32nd Sikh Pioneers (4 companies)
8th Gurkha Rifles (6 companies)
40th Pathans (2 companies)
1st Sappers and Miners (1 company)
1st Mounted Infantry (80 strong)
2nd Mounted Infantry (50 strong)
Norfolk Regiment (Maxim-gun detachment)
Royal Irish Rifles (Maxim-gun detachment)

CHAPTER X

THE MARCH TO LHASA

The force reached Ralung on the 16th, weather wet and cold. Here one company of the 40th and twenty-five of the 3rd Mounted Infantry were left as a garrison. The 1st Mounted Infantry went on to reconnoitre the Karo Là, and as the whole company were together it was possible to drop piquets at two places in it where a small force could have barred our way back. The remainder went on to have a look at the enemy. We found them in their old position, but much strengthened, having built more sangars on the summits of the heights on both sides, and they had built a second wall on a spur in rear of the original wall. Just as we appeared on the scene a large number of their transport yaks were slowly wending their way to the Tibetan position. These were fair prey for the Mounted Infantry, and before the Tibetans knew we were near them or anywhere in the neighbourhood, the Mounted Infantry had dashed down the gorge and rounded up 130 of their baggage yaks and about thirty prisoners. They were driven back about 1,000 yards before the Tibetans were aware of their capture. It made them very angry when they did discover it, and they swarmed up out of their camps to man their walls and sangars, thus giving us a good opportunity of estimating their numbers, which must have been between 4,000 and 5,000. They fired a few shots, but as we did not return them they sat down behind their wall, or began digging to strengthen their position still further.

The yaks were sent back to camp escorted by a Havildar and ten men, and just as they were emerging from the defile of the pass on to the plain a band of Tibetans attempted a rescue, thinking they would overpower the little escort. The Tibetans sprang up out of the rocks, loosed off their guns, and then rushed in sword in hand, but the Havildar and his men (all of the 32nd Pioneers) stood firm, and beyond getting slices of wood slashed out of their rifles suffered no further damage, but they killed six Tibetans and captured ten, whom they marched straight up to the General's tent with the yaks on arrival in camp. The Mounted Infantry piquet, seeing the enemy on the hillside, opened fire on them also, which surprised them so completely that the rest of them decamped, otherwise it might have gone hard with the Havildar and his men. There was a piercingly chill wind blowing on the Tibetan side of the pass that day, and it was bitterly cold work sitting in observation of the Tibetans till dark. We got back to camp at 9.30 P.M., having done twenty-eight miles; the poor ponies were only to be given three pounds of fodder that night.

On the 17th the force marched into the Karo Là defile and camped on the same ground as Colonel Brander's force on May 5. The glacier was still the same, and had not been decreased by the warmer weather.

The General, accompanied by all his commanding officers and Staff, went in the afternoon to view the Tibetan position in person, and make a plan of attack. The 2nd Mounted Infantry were in observation that day, and were highly tried by the cold wind.

The plan of attack formulated was this: Two companies of Gurkhas, under Major Row, were to scale the heights on the left, where he had gone before, and drive the Tibetans out of the sangars. Two companies of Gurkhas, under Major Murray, were to ascend the heights on the right, and evict the enemy from that stronghold. The Royal Fusiliers were to go down the bed of the stream, and make a direct attack on the main wall, supported by the 32nd Sikh Pioneers. The 40th Pathans were in reserve. The guns and Maxims were to prepare and support the attack with their fire. The 1st and 2nd Mounted Infantry were to be in readiness to pursue on the first opportunity. The Gurkhas were allowed three hours to get up the heights, and when near the summits they looked no bigger than an army of ants on the march, which showed the tremendous height they had ascended.

About 9 A.M. the general advance took place, and the Royal Fusiliers reached the wall without any opposition, the enemy having bolted. What a difference from May 6! The Gurkhas up in the clouds on the right were meeting with some opposition, as was evinced by the jingal and rifle fire of their opponents. The Tibetans were holding the numerous caves just under the snowfield, and the Gurkhas were engaged in turning them out, and lost one man killed and two wounded. About 1,000 of the enemy were seen crossing the snowfield beyond, as it was their only way to escape, and the 40th Pathans were sent after them. It was a long climb, but the Pathans enjoyed it. As soon as the Fusiliers gained the wall the 1st Mounted Infantry were sent forward in pursuit, and came up with small parties of the enemy a short way beyond the village which they held on May 6, eight miles from the pass, where their stores and camp were burnt. A Mounted Infantry piquet was left in this village and the remainder went on. The Tibetans met with did their best to escape, and many of them were captured. We went on then to within a couple of miles of Nangartse Jong, the Mounted Infantry advanced guard encountering about 100 Tibetan mounted men, whom they quickly sent flying into the friendly cover of the jong. This place is built on a spur about 100 feet high jutting out on to the plain of the great Yamdok Cho, or Turquoise Lake. It presented a very solid and formidable appearance, but could be commanded from the hills within easy range. Sangars had been built up the spur, and they and the jong were now seen to be occupied, and another fight the following day seemed to be in prospect. The Tibetan prisoners told us that there had been about 5,000 men on the Karo Là on the 16th, but they had lost heart at the capture of Gyantse Jong, and when they saw our force they considered discretion the better part of valour and left.

The most remarkable feature in this day's operations was the altitude at which the fighting took place. The pass itself is 16,200 feet high, and the 8th Gurkhas and 40th Pathans pursued the enemy up to about 19,000 feet, thus creating a record which has not been reached by any army of any nation throughout history, and is now open to the armies of the world to beat. The feats of Hannibal and Napoleon in leading their armies over the Alps (unopposed) have been regarded as the greatest examples of mountain-climbing, but they have been eclipsed by this little British force, who climbed and fought quite 6,000 feet higher. As far as the 1st Mounted Infantry were concerned, it was the last fight in which they were to take part, the last gallop after the enemy, and the last shot they would fire at them. They did not know it at the time, and it was just as well, as the knowledge would have damped their spirits considerably.

The Mission and Force camped that night at Zara, 16,000 eet above sea-level. Next day, the 19th, the force marched on to Nangartse. The 2nd Mounted Infantry were advanced guard, but as resistance was expected at Nangartse, a short time after the force left camp orders arrived for the 1st Mounted In antry to go ahead and support the 2nd. We caught up the 2nd Mounted Infantry close to Nangartse, but instead of their being engaged in action, a very different state of things was in progress. We found Captain Peterson holding a Durbar of his own with the Tibetan Delegates. The Ta Lama, the gentleman with the pain in his stomach, and a new addition, the Yutuk Shapé of the Lhasa Council of State, came out from the jong in great state to meet Captain Peterson, and tell him that if he was good they would hand over the jong to him, and that in the meantime they would not allow any of their stores, ammunition, or armament to be removed. Captain Peterson complied with their request, but took the precaution of sending a section under Captain Souter beyond the jong along the Lhasa road. He had only gone a few miles when he was fired upon by Tibetans, who were trying to get a large convoy away. These Tibetans were undoubtedly armed with modern rifles, but owing to their bad shooting Captain Souter's men escaped uninjured. He captured the whole convoy, and quite a selection of rifles, including the Russian Berdan, Winchesters, Martinis, Lhasa Martinis, Sniders, and Mausers; also a number of revolvers.

The force arrived at Nangartse about 2 P.M. and the jong was occupied at 3 P.M. About 10,000 maunds of grain was found in the jong, which cheered the hearts of the General and poor Major Bretherton. Some fodder was also found. Captain Shepherd and his sappers and miners set to work immediately to remove the powder and construct a defensible post. As the weather had been very wet and the troops were exhausted by long marches and running about on precipitous hillsides 17,000 and 18,000 feet high, the General gave his force a halt next day; and since the Tibetan Delegates, in spite of telling Colonel Younghusband that he should go back to Yatung to carry on negotiations, were very humble, time was thus available to pay a visit to the monastery of the famous Abbess of Tibet. The Samding monastery, where this female incarnation holds her sway, is situated on the east bank of the Yamdok Cho, standing by itself about 300 feet above the lake. The Diamond Sow, or Lady Abbess, is to be congratulated on her choice of position for her earthly residence. It was this good lady at this very place who showed such kindness to the enterprising explorer Serat Chandra Dass over twenty years before, when he arrived there very ill. For further information about this interesting lady and monastery, Serat Chandra Dass's book, page 131, and Markham's 'Tibet,' page 105, should be consulted.

No more beautiful scene can be presented to the eyes of man than the Yamdok Cho and its surrounding hills, as seen by us in the middle of July. There is nothing comparable with the smooth and lovely turquoise-blue waters of this enormous lake set off by the greensward which covers the gently sloping hills on all sides, with Nangartse Jong and Pehte Jong, resembling old Norman castles, reflected in the waters of the lake, on which thousands of the bar-headed goose, with their troops of goslings, were lazily floating about regardless of the white sportsman. This beautiful lake and all its surroundings would be the tourist's ideal resort in summer.

While one company of the 40th and twenty of the 2nd Mounted Infantry were left at Nangartse, the force was to march to Pehte Jong on the 21st, but as the distance was found to be over eighteen miles, and the day was very wet, the General halted four miles short of it. The 1st Mounted Infantry were advanced guard, and were directed to send a patrol down the Rong Chu road where it branched off from the Pehte Jong road and also to reconnoitre Pehte Jong. We arrived at the latter place about two hours after the retreating Tibetan army and the Kham warriors had marched out. It being a very strong place and so easily taken possession of, a message was sent back to the General Officer Commanding asking permission to remain there for the night. This was granted, and, in addition, we were ordered if possible to reconnoitre the Khamba Là and Do Là Passes, 16,000 feet in height.

It rained furiously, but after we had got all the men and ponies settled down in safety, and the Rong Chu patrol had joined us, Major Wallace Dunlop, the energetic brigade signalling officer, and myself spent a very comfortable night in the topmost room of the jong overlooking the lake. Next day we pushed on to reconnoitre the two passes, and determined to see the Brahmaputra River, the crossing of which was such a serious business for the force.

About four miles from Pehte Jong we came on another Tibetan fortified position, which exemplified their extraordinary aptitude for building. In four days the Tibetans had built a five-foot loopholed wall extending from the waters of the lake right up to the top of the Do Là, and yet abandoned it that morning before we arrived. It was a pity they did so, otherwise it would have afforded General Macdonald the opportunity of combining naval and military operations over 15,000 feet above the sea. The General had brought a few Berthon boats for the crossing of the Brahmaputra; these had been launched on the lake, and if the Tibetans had held the wall nothing would have been easier than to put a couple of Maxims into the boats, and then, after sending them down the centre of the lake far out of range, to bring them up and open fire on the Tibetans in rear. On reaching the village at the foot of the Khamba Là, we found it had been looted by the retreating Tibetans, and were told they had passed through during the night. We had now to climb up about 2,000 feet in little over a mile to get to the top of the pass, and from there we saw the long-looked-for Brahmaputra River down in the valley nine miles off. We helioed this information to the General at Pehte Jong and asked for permission to bivouac for the night on the pass, but were directed to get as much information as possible and to return to camp that night, as the Do Là Pass, practically between us and the General, was still reported to be occupied. We were eighteen miles in front when this message was sent and the reply received. We went down the pass about four miles and had a good look at the Brahmaputra Valley, which turned out to be a wealthy, cultivated valley, covered as far as the eye could reach with waving fields of barley, peas, and wheat fit to cut, and dotted all over with villages and monasteries nestling in groves of peach, apricot, and walnut trees. We could see also the two ferries over the river, one at Porte, to the north-west of us, and the other at Chaksam, to the north-east. At both ferries Tibetan hide boats were plying vigorously, carrying across the retreating army, and at Chaksam we could see two large wooden barges lying at anchor. The most important fact of all was that the river was only about 100 to 150 yards wide, in spite of the current information that it was up to 1,000 yards wide. The enemy had built towers and sangars on the opposite bank at Porte Ferry, expecting the force to come over the Do Là and attempt a crossing at Porte. They did not defend Chaksam Ferry nor the Khamba Là leading to it.

What a relief it must have been to Colonel Younghusband and General Macdonald to hear that this bogey of a river was not so formidable as reported, and that there was plenty of flour, fodder, and grain for the force in a few days, as well as abundant material available to aid in the crossing of the Brahmaputra! It was a great pleasure to my company and myself that we had the privilege of having seen this great river first. In fact, we were the immediate successors of Mr. Manning, who made his way to Lhasa, unhelped by the Indian Government, and crossed the Brahmaputra at the reach now under our view, ninety-four years before.

We got back to camp at about 9 P.M., having covered forty miles, climbed up 2,000 feet, descended 3,000 feet, and repeated the same inversely on the way back. Next day the force, leaving one company 40th and twenty of the 2nd Mounted Infantry to garrison Pehte Jong, marched along the edge of the lake and camped at the foot of the Khamba Là. The 2nd Mounted Infantry were advanced guard, and spent most of the day in observation on top of the pass. After camp had been pitched, the fishermen in the force were busy trying their luck in the Yamdok Cho. The most successful was Mr. Magniac, Colonel Younghusband's private secretary, who caught a fine fish weighing six pounds, of a species totally unknown to anglers or naturalists. The General's scheme for the 24th was that the 1st and 2nd Mounted Infantry should march on the Brahmaputra with all possible speed and seize all the boats on the river between Porte and Chaksam Ferries, and that the force should follow on, cross the pass, and camp as near as possible to the river.

Major Iggulden, the C.S.O., took command of the two companies of Mounted Infantry, and, accompanied by Captains Shepherd and Elliott, R.E., we started early. It was impossible to ride down the pass as it was so steep, falling 5,000 feet in eight miles, which took us over two hours to walk down. Half the 2nd Mounted Infantry, under Captain Souter, were sent to Porte Ferry, and the rest of us went on to Chaksam. Passing through the barley-fields on the way, a badger was started, and was immediately chased by those officers who had swords. Captain Elliot, inflicting a slight wound, drew first blood. It was a good opportunity for the men to try their fixed bayonets on horseback, so three of them and myself with rifles and fixed bayonets joined in the chase. Luck was with me, and the badger's *coup de grâce* was given by a vigorous thrust with the bayonet.

On arrival at Chaksam we found no enemy, but the barges and boats were carefully moored at the far side of the river. The guide directed us to the Palchen Churori monastery, about half a mile below the ferry. The poor people and monks, having been looted and harassed by the retreating Tibetan army, had nearly all fled. The river is here spanned by the remains of a chain suspension bridge over 400 years old. Only the chains now remained, and it was therefore impassable. After

CHAKSAM FERRY, WITH THE REMAINS OF AN IRON CHAIN SUSPENSION BRIDGE.

some delay one of the chief Lamas and several of his boatmen were discovered. They were very frightened, and expected that we would treat them in the same way as their own countrymen. However, their confidence was soon restored, and they were ready to put all their boats at our disposal; but, pointing to the retreating army on the opposite side of the river, now not more than one mile off, they said, 'Protect us from those vagabonds, and we will do anything for you.' Major Iggulden and the 2nd Mounted Infantry returned to the General's camp, leaving us to guard the ferry, monastery, and boats for the night and have everything ready for crossing in the morning. The Lama was told that he would get ten rupees a day for each of his big boats, and that his boatmen would get two rupees a day each, and that if he helped us willingly and well I would ask the General to give a present of 200 rupees to his monastery. They did not believe us, of course, nor did they think it possible that we would pay this, to them, enormous wage for boats and labour. The Lama and about twenty boatmen were then brought down to the ferry, together with two skin boats found hidden under the monastery bank of the river. I showed them twenty rupees and told them that they were theirs if they brought the two barges to our side of the river; but no, they would not trust us, and were too much afraid of their own people. Well, there was nothing left but to tell them they had got to do it, and that we would shoot anybody who attempted to interfere with them. The river here was flowing at about seven miles an hour, a very treacherous stream, and it was wonderful the way they navigated their apparently unsteerable skin boat across. In half an hour we had the barges at our side and the twenty men safe in our camp. It was raining hard, and they begged to be let go to the monastery and promised to come back next morning, but this, of course, could not be agreed to. I gave them their twenty rupees, and told the Lama to send me ten sheep, some tsampa and chung (country beer) for the boatmen, for which he would be paid. This won their hearts, and in a short time they produced ten more skin boats, which they brought on shore and, turning them upside down, converted them into capital waterproof tents, which sheltered them and nearly all the men for the night. Everybody was now happy, especially the Mounted Infantry men, as they were able to cut as much green barley as the ponies could eat, and although we had no kits or tents that night, they being saturated with rain when they did turn up, yet we had reached the Brahmaputra and would cross next day—a fact sufficient to keep everybody in good spirits and make them forget discomforts.

By 8 o'clock next morning, July 25, the 1st Mounted Infantry were across the river, and had occupied several villages on the other side and were patrolling in all directions. Remnants of the fleeing army were again seen, but our orders were to leave them alone if they did not fire on us. By evening two companies of the 40th and five companies of the 8th had crossed, and Colonel Campbell took command of the whole. The success of this day was marred by a sad and unexpected accident. The Berthon boats were working splendidly, both separately and in pairs united by a platform which converted them into a raft. Major Bretherton, D.S.O., Captain Moore, 4th Lancers, and eight Gurkhas were crossing on one of these rafts, when, one of the boats getting swamped, the raft overturned, precipitating all its occupants into the eddying waters of the Brahmaputra. They were all wearing their heavy warm clothes and equipment, and out of the party Captain Moore and five Gurkhas saved themselves with the greatest difficulty; three of the Gurkhas holding on to their rifles, risked their lives to save them, and were successful in their effort. Bretherton and three Gurkhas, having got wide of the Berthon boat, which, being buoyant, did not sink, were immediately engulfed by the surging waters and were never seen again. It was a sad loss. Poor Bretherton, who for the past ten months had worked like a slave to supply and anticipate all our wants, was now, when we wanted him more than ever, and when he would have had the satisfaction of seeing his labours crowned with success, cut off from us for ever. To be killed in action is every good soldier's ideal, and a death in that way does not leave behind it a gloom of sadness; but to be the victim of a cruel fate, as Major Bretherton was, caused heartfelt regret to all those who knew him and had served with him.

To hasten and facilitate the crossing of about 10,000 maunds, about 4,000 men, and over 4,500 animals (the river being too dangerously rapid to swim the animals), more boats were required. On the 26th, therefore, all who were left of the 1st Mounted Infantry not engaged in patrolling—namely, myself and sixteen men—started off to get mutton, beef, fodder, and boats. We had no difficulty in getting the first three, as the inhabitants, under a show of force to save their reputations with their own people, were willing to sell supplies. Eight men were detailed to take back to camp some 200 sheep, fifty cows, and lots of fodder. The look of delight on the poor Tibetans' faces when they were given about 4,000 rupees for these supplies was indescribable. They were unaccustomed to this kind of treatment. To get boats was a more difficult matter; they being few in number, such as there were had been removed

TROOPS CROSSING AT CHAKSAM FERRY.

from the river and hidden. A very respectable old Tibetan gave us a hint as to where boats might be found. The place was fifteen miles off up the river towards the great gorge through which the Brahmaputra bursts from the Shigatse plain. We passed through a very pretty, well-cultivated country, in which there were many well-to-do villages, nearly all of which had been ransacked by the Tibetan army, and the inhabitants, thinking we would do the same or worse, had fled to the hills. At length we passed a village the people of which came out to see us, bringing presents of eggs, frozen mutton, and fire in earthenware vessels, the highest mark of honour and respect. We stopped and talked, and drank quantities of buttered tea, which I would have given a great deal not to have touched, but that it would have been discourteous to refuse. When we explained to them what we wanted, saying that the boats would be paid for, and that anybody pointing them out would be well rewarded, a man volunteered to come and show us boats. He was an excellent fellow, and took us straight to a village about a mile and a half from the river in which twenty-seven fine skin boats were hidden. The only drawback was that, the village being deserted, there was nobody to take the boats to the river, and not a human being could be found in the country round. We lay low in the village in the hope that somebody would turn up, and after a bit five of the opposing army, not suspecting our presence, walked into the village. These were immediately made to shoulder a boat each and carry them down to the river. Four Mounted Infantry men also carried down a couple of boats. We had got thirteen boats in the water just as it fell dark, and at 7.30 P.M. we decided it would be better to get these to Chaksam Ferry without waiting to bring down any more.

A Tibetan skin boat is a most difficult craft to manage, and would puzzle any 'Varsity oarsman. The river was very swift, and none of the Tibetans were boatmen, nor were we expert enough to row them down the river. Under the circumstances the safest plan to get the boats along was to tie them all together stem to stern, with ropes from the first and thirteenth boat to the shore, each of which was held on to by the Tibetans and Mounted Infantry men. The flotilla started at 7.30 P.M., and having toiled all night, with many vicissitudes, we arrived at Chaksam Ferry at 6.30 the following morning, having been going exactly twenty-four hours without food except a few barley-flour chupatties (cakes), and without a stop. It was a hard night's work, but was not without its amusing incidents. When we came to streams and rivulets flowing into the Brahmaputra, these had to be waded across by the whole party, including the men holding on to the ropes. Some of these streams were deep, and the Tibetans at the best of times dislike water, but when they were asked to go into anything above two feet deep they became terrified. One place was about five feet deep, and they absolutely preferred to risk the threats of being shot than to face it. It had to be crossed all the same. I found a shallower place, too far from the main river for the ropes to reach, and then crossed and waded in from the opposite side to meet the Tibetans, who were being hustled in by the Mounted Infantry men. This gave them confidence, especially when they saw that I was able to stand up all right in water up to my neck, so they came along shouting with terror, and when they reached me out of sheer fright three of them hung on to me, and we were all near being carried down the river. We got across all right, however, and when they found themselves safe they were very jubilant, and laughed and sang songs, and were very pleased with themselves till they came to the next bit of water to be crossed, when they immediately lapsed into dead silence.

The Tibetan interpreter was full of zeal until half the night was passed, when he became very sleepy, and seized the opportunity, when delay was caused by the crossing of a difficult place, to lie down and go to sleep. Several times we had to go back for him and kick him hard to wake him up, for it was essential, on his account as well as our own, that he should not be left behind.

With the arrival of the additional boats on the 28th the crossing of the force was much facilitated, and the General was able to give out that the whole force would be across the river on the 30th, and that he would commence the march to Lhasa on the 31st. Beef and mutton for the troops were nearly run out, so I was directed to find and bring in what I could. The local people, having been looted by their own army, and fearing we would do the same, had driven all their flocks and herds far up into the hills. They would not point them out or sell them to us through fear of the Lhasa authorities. Early on the morning of the 29th we started on a foraging expedition, and returned to camp next day at 2 A.M. with 1,700 sheep and forty-four cows. The owners were brought in also, and they did look pleased when they were handed over the first bag of rupees containing 1,000. They thought this was enough payment, and were about to go away quite satisfied, but when they were given about 6,500 more they did not seem to know what to do with it. It made them forget their own dreads and the commands of the Lhasa authorities, as they brought in abundant supplies afterwards. During this day's work the showa (or Tibetan stag) were sighted on a treeless

MR. PERCIVAL LANDON, OF THE 'TIMES,' LEAVING CHAKSAM FOR LHASA.

hillside, although in the Chumbi Valley only found in thick jungle. One company of the 40th and twenty-two of the 1st Mounted Infantry were left at Chaksam.

There was great rejoicing in the rest of the force on the morning of July 31, when the march to Lhasa was commenced. It was only forty-seven miles away now, and it held out prospects either of fighting or of peace and plenty. About five miles from our camp we passed Chu Shul Jong and ridge, a position of prodigious natural strength. It had been sangared and covered with defensive walls to oppose our advance, but the Tibetans had abandoned it the first day we crossed the Brahmaputra. A few miles further on we got into the Kyi Chu Valley, in which stands Lhasa. It is a fine open valley, well cultivated and very productive, with numbers of snug-looking villages, and residences surrounded with groves of trees.

The poor old Ta Lama was in a terrible state of mind at our advance, and used to argue daily with Colonel Younghusband about the wickedness and futility of going to Lhasa. He was really trying to gain time to allow the Dalai Lama and his Russian tutor Dorjieff to get well clear of Lhasa before our arrival, and also he was seriously perturbed about the safety of his own head at the hands of the Tibetans. On August 1 the 1st Mounted Infantry were advanced guard, and, accompanied by Major Iggulden, the C.S.O., we were determined to see Lhasa that day.

As we went on the valley became wider and wider and more and more fertile, the road leading through magnificent crops. Two hundred and twenty grains of corn were counted in one head. We caught up the Ta Lama and his retinue, who halted in order once more to endeavour by argument to overcome Colonel Younghusband. They said Lhasa could be seen from a distant ridge apparently blocking the road. To this ridge we determined to go. It was only twelve miles from Lhasa, about 700 feet high, very steep, and very difficult going. The crisis had now come. Who should see Lhasa first? British officers, Sikhs, and Gurkhas, all alike were madly keen, each one to claim for himself that honour; so, having dismounted at the foot of the ridge, all but the horse-holders and the guard commenced a race up that hill which I can never forget, and should be sorry to have to do over again. Major Iggulden was so uncommonly good on a hillside that for quite three-quarters of the way he looked very like winning. The hard going and the pace now began to tell on him, and gradually I myself and some of the men drew away. Finally the 150 rounds on the men as against my fifty rounds enabled me to get to the top first, but I must confess I was so blown that I could not see twelve yards, much less

DISTANT VIEW OF LHASA CITY.

twelve miles. Lhasa was now really before us, and a very small portion of it was visible. The Wizard's Shrine, with its golden roof, near the great Debong monastery, and the Sara monastery, north of Lhasa, were clearly seen. We had ridden out about twenty-two miles, and had to return ten to camp, so we did not delay long on the ridge. At the foot of this ridge is the largest image of Buddha in the whole of Tibet, carved in rock and quite 80 feet high. Next day, the 2nd Mounted Infantry were advanced guard, and the force marched to Trelung Bridge, six miles from Lhasa. This is a fine stone bridge about 16 feet wide and 130 yards long; it crosses the Ti Chu, a tributary of the Kyi Chu. In the afternoon all the chief Lamas of the surrounding monasteries and several Tibetan men of rank and position came to see Colonel Younghusband. They were all mounted on splendid ponies or mules, which the Mounted Infantry men really coveted. The ruling Lama of Debong monastery told Colonel Younghusband that he had 10,000 armed monks under him, and if the force advanced further towards Lhasa he could not be responsible should they attack our force and eat us up. It was explained to them that we were rather fine-drawn from hard marching and poor rations, and that they would therefore find us rather tough eating. They left camp very haughty and angry, and resistance was expected the following day, when we should march to Lhasa.

Fifty Gurkhas and five of the 1st Mounted Infantry were left in a defensible post to guard the Trelung Bridge, and the remainder of the force, now reduced to 130 Mounted Infantry, eight guns, 1,450 infantry and sappers, and six Maxims, marched to Lhasa on August 3, 1904, and camped on an open grassy plain near the Kota Ling, or Dalai Lama's summer palace.

The Tongsa Pendlop of Butan and his following started off with a great flourish of trumpets in front of the whole force, but on getting near Lhasa he thought better of it, distrusting the Tibetans, and allowed the 1st Mounted Infantry, who were the advanced guard, to go in front of him, and followed them at some distance. We marched on without any incident, passing the great Debong monastery, outside which several thousand monks had assembled; but they had evidently lost their appetites, as they did not attempt to attack us. The next place of importance was the Oracle House, with its shining golden roof. From this point the general view of the Lhasa plain was at its best. The Chagpori, or medical college, stands on the summit of an eminence near the Kyi Chu, connected by a col with the eminence on which the stately Potala stands, and further again to the left the Sara monastery. All these buildings,

THE CHAGPORI, OR MEDICAL COLLEGE, AT LHASA.

with their gilded roofs, were strikingly imposing. The road now led across a fine grassy plain, the greater part of which is swamp, off which the Dalai Lama has his grass cut for winter use. The actual city of Lhasa was not yet visible. Our orders were that we should not go into it, but observe it from some place where we could get a satisfactory view and choose a good defensible position from which Lhasa city could be easily overawed. This choice is easy, as there is only one—that between Potala and Chagpori, where the col or ridge in the centre almost dips to the level of the plain, and at the lowest part of which is a fine gateway. Having arrived here, we dismounted and ascended the ridge on our right towards the Chagpori. From here the whole of Lhasa city was suddenly exposed to view, lying at our feet, about 1,200 yards off. It looked exquisite: the trees in full leaf, the gilt roofs of the Jo-Khang and king's palace glittering in the sun, the greensward, well planted with shrubs, through which rivulets meandered, in whose quiet waters thousands of small fish were basking. Little wonder, it flashed across us, if the Tibetans wished to keep their chief city secluded from the prying, curious world. The inhabitants paid no attention to us, and continued their usual occupations, as if the appearance of a foreign force was an every-day occurrence. Lieutenant

Bailey commenced fishing in one of the rivulets, and was soon the centre of admiration to a number of Tibetan men and women, who greeted each successful capture of a fish with loud laughter. Soon numbers of officers of the force and the correspondents came up to our place on the ridge to see the now no longer Forbidden City. In the afternoon the Chinese Amban, with a gorgeous retinue, paid a state visit to Colonel Younghusband, and presented the troops with the donation of a herd of sheep, some cattle, wheaten flour, and 4,000 tankas (about 1,300 rupees).

There was nobody more pleased at the arrival of the British force at Lhasa than the Amban, as he had been living in fear and trembling among the Tibetans, and now felt safe.

THE POTALA AND ENVIRONS OF LHASA.

CHAPTER XI

AT LHASA

THE next day Colonel Younghusband, escorted by the 2nd Mounted Infantry and about three hundred rifles, returned the Amban's visit, after which he marched through the whole of the city and was everywhere received with wondering respect. In the afternoon he was visited by a large body of Tibetan officials, but owing to their perseverance in their obstinacy, nothing in the way of a settlement could be arrived at, and they had the impertinence to talk of the difficulties they had in restraining the Tibetan army, distributed in places some miles from Lhasa, from attacking us.

They were as proud and stubborn as ever, and did not consider themselves in the least degree conquered, nor were they at all inclined to make a treaty. They promised supplies on payment. These were to be furnished by the Lamas of the great monasteries. They failed to carry out their promises till forced to do so by General Macdonald.

On the 6th the Nepaulese agent paid a state

visit to Colonel Younghusband, and gave the troops a present of 4,000 tankas.

Both the Amban, who is a most polished gentleman, and other local authorities said that the Tibetan state officials were the most impossible people to deal with, and to bring them to a practical and businesslike state of mind they should have their heads beaten on the ground. The Amban also stated that he placed no reliance in the Tibetans' promises to bring in supplies, and that they would not do so unless compelled, as they hoped to reduce the British force to a weak state by starvation and then attack. Such was the character of the men Colonel Younghusband had to carry on negotiations with, and it redounds all the more to his credit that from such men he eventually obtained the best terms ever got by a frontier political officer since the Mutiny.

On the 7th General Macdonald, with a large escort, called on the Amban in Lhasa, and was most courteously received by the diplomatically capable representative of China. Rations were now at the last ebb, and the Tibetans showed no signs of bringing in supplies. The General with unalterable patience gave them every chance of fulfilling their promises. Not being able to do without rations any longer, on the 8th he took out a column of about 900 rifles and six guns against the Debong monastery to impress on the Lamas

MONKS AT THE SARA MONASTERY.

the fact that they were expected to fulfil their promises of supplying rations. A letter was taken to them by Captain O'Connor, escorted by a few of the 2nd Mounted Infantry. The monks would not receive this letter, and were grossly insulting to Captain O'Connor, and finally threw stones at him and his escort. Notwithstanding this outrageous provocation General Macdonald, still patient, did not retaliate by force of arms, but sent a message that he would give them two hours to bring out 1,000 maunds of grain. They could have produced fifty times that amount.

The monks treated this message also with contempt, and it was not till the guns were in position to open fire, and the infantry actually advancing to the attack, that they commenced to bring out grain, for which they were instantly paid in cash. The column then withdrew, and the Lamas again lapsed into lethargy, and for the next few days brought in nothing. On the 9th the 1st Mounted Infantry under the supervision of Major Beynon, D.S.O., escorted Captain O'Connor, bearing a letter of requisition for supplies to the Sara monastery. Several thousand monks formed up outside the monastery to receive us, and were quite hostile in their aspect. The Mounted Infantry were dismounted and placed in position about 400 yards from the monastery to cover the handing-over of the letter.

Major Beynon, Captain O'Connor, and myself with three men advanced towards the monks, while in like fashion six or eight of the head Lamas came out to meet us. At first they were quite insolent and would not take the letter, but Captain O'Connor in a few words to the point induced them to assume a more friendly frame of mind, and taking the letter of requisition, they promised to bring in supplies in a few days.

A Mounted Infantry piquet under a native officer was daily posted on the road between the camp and Lhasa city near the Kota Ling Palace, and on one particular occasion proved of excellent service, and most probably prevented a terrible catastrophe.

On the 10th Colonel Younghusband, escorted by the 1st Mounted Infantry, was to pay a political visit to the Amban in Lhasa. A short time after Colonel Younghusband had passed the Mounted Infantry piquet on his way to the city, they saw a suspicious-looking Lama, carrying a curiously long bundle wrapped up in cloth, sneaking about in the brushwood near the road. Some men went towards him, and he tried to escape, but was quickly captured. On opening the bundle they found a loaded musket hidden away, and there is no doubt his intention, thus happily frustrated, was to shoot Colonel Younghusband on his way back to camp.

COLONEL YOUNGHUSBAND AND M.I. ESCORT RETURNING FROM LHASA.

This Lama, with other prisoners, was taken out next day to cut grass for the ponies near the Debong monastery, under an escort of a few Mounted Infantry men. While thus employed the Lama seized an opportunity of making a dash for liberty, and bolted for a body of about five hundred Lamas who had come out of the monastery to look at their friends cutting grass for the British. A Gurkha Sepoy named Rundle Rana, in whose charge the Lama was, perceiving this retrograde movement on the part of the Lama, gave chase, and seeing that the Lama would gain the large number of his fraternity before he could catch him, fired his rifle, aiming high enough to let the bullet pass unpleasantly near their heads. This was too much for the Lamas, and they hastily dispersed, driving their offending brother out from their midst. The latter, having divested himself of most of his clothes, made for the hills, with the little Gurkha in hot pursuit. The Gurkha, thinking the Lama might escape, dropped on his knee, took aim, and fired, hitting him on the thigh. The wound was a flesh one, but sufficient to make the Lama slacken his speed. As the Lama found himself overhauled he pelted the Gurkha with stones, and finally, throwing himself—being a big, powerful man—on the Gurkha, rolled with him some way down the hill. The Gurkha then drew his bayonet and smote the Lama on the head, which knocked all the fight out of him.

I was fishing on the far side of the Kyi Chu, about 800 yards away, just opposite where this fracas took place, and hearing the shots, saw all that took place without being able to recognise the parties concerned; but, perceiving that something unusual was going on, went back with my companions to camp—for that was the only accessible way—and then on towards the monastery, when we met the gallant little Gurkha with his rifle loaded, his bayonet fixed, and beaming all over with delight, bringing in his now tame and wounded Lama prisoner.

It is extraordinary what great results some little incidents have, as happened in this case. The determined behaviour of the Gurkha, and the letting of blood, under the very eyes of the large body of Lamas, acted like magic on their hitherto sullen behaviour, their passive resistance to orders, and breaking of promises to bring in supplies.

The following day the Lamas of Debong brought in 1,500 maunds of supplies, the Sara monastery also sent 1,000, and both monasteries for the future worked assiduously to complete their requisitions.

The weather having been very wet for some days past, our camp was immersed in six inches to a foot of water, and a dry day was being anxiously

DEBONG MONASTERY, WITH THE ORACLE HOUSE ON THE RIGHT.

waited for to shift camp to a drier site north of Lhasa between the Potala and Sara monastery.

On the 12th camp was shifted to the new site, which, although sandy and dry on top, had water three feet below the surface.

Colonel Younghusband and the Mission, escorted by two companies of the 40th Pathans, took up their residence in the Lalu Palace, a large and well-built house with courtyard. Our new camp was a decided improvement on the old, but was terribly rheumatic and trying. It was here, then, that we had to sit and wait for the Tibetans to make up their minds to sign a treaty or not.

The representatives of the Tibetan Government were constantly threatening Colonel Younghusband with the difficulty they had in restraining their army, still in the neighbourhood, from attacking us. General Macdonald also had received intelligence of large numbers of the enemy being located in various places, and early on the morning of the 12th he directed me to take as many of my company as I could and reconnoitre the Pemba Là Pass, about fifteen miles north-east of Lhasa. Owing to various other patrols and duties having to be provided for, I could only muster one native officer and twenty-three men, and with these, accompanied by Mr. Heydon, the geologist, proceeded to explore still further into Tibet. We were quite certain also that, although

Manning and some French priests had visited Lhasa, no white man or native of India had ever been on the Pemba Là.

Proceeding up the Lhasa Valley, we rounded a spur east of the Sara monastery and entered another rich valley covered with luxuriant fields of corn. About four miles up, the valley divides into two, one going north-east and the other north. We followed the latter, which soon became narrower and narrower, and steeper and steeper. On the way we passed the spot where the Tibetans cut up their dead and throw the pieces to the birds of the air and the beasts of the field. Further on was a Chinese joss-house, and at about six miles the new Tibetan Mint, which had just been built for the purposes of a new coinage. The machinery had not yet been put in, and most probably never will be now. Having met several people on the road, we asked them if the enemy were in the vicinity, and they invariably replied that they never heard of any, although there were about 600 or 800 of them only three miles off. The valley became rapidly narrower and steeper till from a distance it seemed blocked by a solid wall of rock. On closer view it takes a sharp turn to the right, and here the gorge between two huge walls of rock is only 100 feet wide, and the road running up steps of rock is only six feet broad, passing along the edge of a precipice at the bottom

1ST M.I. MESS AT LHASA: MR. CANDLER, MAJOR WALLACE DUNLOP, AND CAPTAIN OTTLEY (R. TO L.); LIEUT. BAILEY AND LIEUT. RYBAT.

of which dashes a raging, foaming torrent, the whole forming a most extraordinary *cul-de-sac*. The advanced Mounted Infantry scouts had hardly entered the narrowest part of the road when they sent me word that they had captured a Tibetan piquet of two soldiers, whom they surprised asleep. On hearing this we all dismounted, and rushing up to the scouts, gathered from the prisoners that there was a large force of the enemy close at hand. The ponies and prisoners were left amongst the boulders, and Mr. Heydon, armed with a revolver and his well-known hammer, myself, and eighteen rifles, half Sikhs, half Gurkhas, hurried on up the gorge.

As soon as the defile opened out an extraordinary sight met our view. There were five large Tibetan tents full of soldiers, scattered about. The Tibetans were all gambling or napping, and thoroughly enjoying themselves, in sublime ignorance that a Mounted Infantry patrol was anywhere near them. We had rushed past the first two tents before being discovered, when the Tibetans made a dash for their swords and guns; but when they saw a number of our rifles levelled at them, and were told that if they did anything they would be shot, they elected to do nothing. Six men were left under the native officer to overawe them, and the rest of us ran on to the other three tents, which were pitched just below the road. Before the

Tibetans could move, our rifles were levelled at them twenty yards off, and they also, seeing they were at a disadvantage, gave themselves up. Their hands were tied behind their backs, their swords, guns, and rifles slung on their shoulders, and they were hurried down the gorge beyond the ponies. The cliffs on the opposite side of the stream, which is here less rapid, were honeycombed with caves. Having with great difficulty crossed the stream, we instituted a search of these caves, which resulted in the capture of several more prisoners and quantities of gunpowder, which was flung into the water. We then went higher up the valley, which had somewhat opened out, and about one mile further on we saw the main Tibetan camp, in which there must have been 600 to 800 men. Having already sixty-four prisoners and twelve ponies and mules to guard, and only six rifles left, we could not grapple with the main camp, so started on our return journey to camp. Our total bag was sixty-four prisoners, twelve ponies, sixty-seven guns and rifles, and forty-seven swords. The men were hugely delighted with their success, and their spirits only fell for a moment when passing the rock on which the corpses are cut up, for there now two Lamas were busily engaged in the performance of this ghastly ceremony, surrounded by hundreds of vultures and scores of dogs, which were eating up the pieces of flesh thrown to them,

1ST M.I. IN THE LHASA MARKET PLACE.

or gnawing the pieces of broken bone which one of the Lamas was smashing up by lifting a great rock above his head, and dropping it on the bones. It was a horrid sight, and the natives of India expressed their disgust very strongly.

It was most fortunate that the Chinese Amban and several of the Tibetan high officials were in camp when the procession of prisoners arrived there. The effect of the capture on these gentlemen was curious to watch. The Amban did not restrain his pleasure, and expressed himself well satisfied that the bogey of the Tibetan army had thus been exploded. The Tibetan gentlemen were decidedly crestfallen, and in their ensuing interviews with Colonel Younghusband, they did not again bring forward the threat of their voracious army thirsting for our blood.

On reporting to the General the position of the main body of the Tibetan army, he directed me to go out again next day with my full company, and if necessary drive them out of their position. The news of this project spread like wildfire through our camp, and dozens of officers, bored with the long spell of inactivity, and anxious to be in a fight, volunteered, and asked leave to accompany me. The General was adamant, and would not allow anybody to go except Captain Ryder, R.E., who said he must seize the opportunity of the Mounted Infantry escort to survey from the Pemba Là;

Mr. Heydon, who for a like reason said he must find out if there were gold mines or coal mines on top of the same pass; and Mr. Magniac, the sporting private secretary to Colonel Younghusband. I am not sure if he had leave or not, but in any case he came.

The company mustered Lieutenant Bailey and sixty rifles, and all were pleased at the prospect of having a brush with the enemy.

We arrived at their camp about 8 A.M.; but, alas! they had gone. The capture of the previous day was too much for them, and they thought that they would be safer thirty or forty miles further away from Lhasa. We pushed on, and after two hours of a very steep climb, reached the top of the pass, whence we saw the enemy in full retreat ten miles away down in the next valley. Pursuit was unnecessary, as the G.O.C.'s object had been carried out; he did not want to inflict more losses on the Tibetans, and only wished them to disperse and leave the vicinity of Lhasa.

Although the enemy had escaped us, we were well rewarded in the magnificent view obtained from the pass. Imagine the centre of a circle with a radius of from 70 to 150 miles, the circumference of which was a range of mountains varying from 15,000 to 23,000 feet high. On the south could be seen the snow-peaks of the Karo Là, over 22,000 feet high; while on the north,

1ST M.I. MESS AT LHASA. MR. MAGNIAC MOUNTED ON 'THE DEVIL,' HELD BY CAPTAIN MOORE.

Captain Ryder fixed a snow-peak over 23,000, just south of the great Tengri Nur Lake, which had been seen by that intrepid explorer Littledale, when he was surveying in North Tibet, and fixed the position of the Tengri Nur. Captain Ryder was thus able to link up the surveys of Northern Tibet with those of Southern Tibet which he had done himself, thereby, to a certain extent, completing the first survey of that country.

The height of the Pemba Là Pass was fixed at 16,300 feet. We ascended a steep pinnacle on the right of the pass to get a better view; this was well over 18,000 feet, and very cold. Captain Ryder and his men did a couple of hours' sketching, while we sat shivering. Mr. Heydon was unable to find the gold we expected to come across, which depressed yet further our already damped spirits. However, we had spent a very pleasant day.

This was the last event against the enemy in which the 1st Mounted Infantry took part—in fact, it was the closing incident for the Mission force. The 1st and 2nd Mounted Infantry had now for their only excitement the carrying of the mails and 'line-clear' telegrams between Lhasa and Chaksam Ferry on the Brahmaputra, a distance of forty-seven miles. Ten men would start from Lhasa, carrying thirty pounds of mail-bags and a blanket each; they stayed the night at the ferry, and came back next day, bringing the same weight of mails on their saddles. This was done three times a week for seven weeks without ever suffering a hitch of any kind—a march of ninety-four miles in two days, which, I think, will be acknowledged as a most creditable performance for both men and ponies.

The Tibetans had now become much more civil to Colonel Younghusband, and allowed parties of officers to visit all the great monasteries, which were most interesting.

Life at Lhasa now became dull, and gymkhanas, sports, race-meetings, and rifle-meetings were got up to pass the time. Fishing in the Kyi Chu was good, and afforded a great deal of sport and pleasure. Shooting was prohibited for fear of offending the sensitive feelings of the Lamas by the taking of life.

Many people were busy making out schemes for various exploring trips they wished to undertake. Mr. Wilton was hoping to go to Pekin *via* the Kham country in Eastern Tibet and the Yangtse Valley, and two of my Mounted Infantry men were to escort him.

Then there was a party wishing to go back to India through Butan. Another wanted to go from Gyantse to Shigatse, Gartok, and Western Tibet to Simla. This was the only trip that actually came off.

The expedition I was interested in was to go

LHASA RACES: COLONEL YOUNGHUSBAND IN THE JUDGE'S BOX.

down the Brahmaputra Valley, coming out in Assam, to explore and survey that portion of this great river which, although only 150 miles from our Indian frontier, has never been traversed by any human being, with the exception of the unknown wild tribes inhabiting that region, who are said to be cannibals. The expedition was to consist of 200 Gurkhas and five British officers. Had it gone, it would have cleared up that vexed geographical question whether the Brahmaputra at Saiddia in Assam is the same river as that we crossed near Lhasa.

On August 18 the even tenor of our existence at Lhasa was rudely disturbed by a stalwart Lama, who, dressing himself in a suit of chain armour, and concealing two swords under his clothes, walked into camp amongst the Tibetans bringing in supplies, and without any warning made a violent attack on two I.M.S. officers, Captain Kelly and Captain Cook Young, who were both unarmed, inflicting serious wounds on each. A sentry close by charged him with his bayonet; but, owing to the chain armour, the thrust had no effect. The two officers saved their lives by their stout resistance and presence of mind in tackling the fanatic Lama till at length he was laid low by a blow from a Sepoy of the 32nd Sikh Pioneers who happened to be passing by, carrying a pick-axe, from which he quickly withdrew the handle—

a favourite weapon of offence and defence in Pioneer regiments—wherewith he gave the Lama his quietus. General Macdonald had him tried and hanged next day. Colonel Younghusband inflicted a fine of 5,000 rupees on the nearest monastery, which they paid at once—not in cash, as they said it was not convenient, but in rolls of silk, the robes of Tibetan gentlemen and the silk garments of Chinese ladies, which were all accepted at the valuation put on them by the monks. Most of these were sold by auction, and caused much amusement and brisk bidding amongst the officers, especially the ladies' silk petticoats, which were very curious and beautifully worked.

Nothing of importance took place from this on till the morning of September 3, when Colonel Younghusband astounded us all by telling us that the Tibetans had agreed to sign a convention in the sacred Potala Palace on September 7. This great political victory was gained by Colonel Younghusband over the most argumentative and stubborn race of people in the world by his patient tact, splendid ability, and unwearying political zeal. He overcame the Tibetans—who had no intention of signing a convention, in the hope they would starve the Mission and Force into going away—by his diplomacy, firmness, and liberality with them, and without force of arms he won them to his side. In this he was vastly assisted

MOUNTED INFANTRY PREPARED FOR AN OVERLAND JOURNEY TO PEKIN.

by the unimpeachable conduct of all ranks of General Macdonald's force.

The Potala Palace is the place where the sacred picture of the Emperor of China is kept, the desertion of which by the fugitive Dalai Lama caused him to be unfrocked by the Emperor of China. The signing of the Convention there with the concurrence of the Amban made it all the more binding on the Tibetans, and it proved to the whole nation, and to the great annual caravan of Mongolians, including representatives from Mongolia, North China, and Southern Siberia, that the British force had pierced the redoubtable barriers of the Himalayas, overcoming all physical and climatic difficulties, and defeating the Tibetans, and that, without claiming the rights of a conquering army, they were peaceably sitting at Lhasa, paying for their supplies and for any luxuries or other articles they wished to obtain. How different from the treatment dealt out by those very Mongols when they sacked and looted Lhasa nearly 200 years before!

On September 7 all the dignity and solemnity possible was afforded to the signing of the Convention. Both officers and men put on the best khaki they had. The roads up to the audience-hall of the Potala were lined with troops, through which rode Colonel Younghusband and his Staff in political uniform, accompanied by General

Macdonald and his Staff, and escorted by the 1st and 2nd Mounted Infantry, an honour of which the men of those two companies felt very proud.

On arriving at the foot of the steep road leading up to the Potala, the procession dismounted, and, preceded by twelve men of the 1st Mounted Infantry and followed by twelve men of the 2nd Mounted Infantry, these two distinguished men, who had so capably brought the Mission to this successful issue, stepped lightly up the very slippery steps and corridors of the Potala. The stones had become so polished by the feet of the countless Lamas of ages, and were so slippery, that they were dangerous to walk on, and many a Tommy sat harder on them than he intended to, giving vent to his feelings in his own peculiar metaphor. But General Macdonald, who wore a pair of indiarubber snow-boots, was the only one who walked with dignity and safety.

In the audience-hall had assembled the Amban and his Staff, the Nepaulese Resident and his Staff, the Tongsa Pendlop of Butan, the Tibetan Councillors of State and chief Lamas, all dressed in gorgeous garments, who with the handsomely painted and decorated hall formed a most brilliant spectacle. Refreshments having been passed round, the proceedings were commenced, and conducted by Colonel Younghusband in English, translated to the Tibetans by Captain O'Connor, and retrans-

TIBETAN ENTERTAINMENT GIVEN TO COLONEL YOUNGHUSBAND.

lated from Tibetan to Chinese for the Amban by a Chinaman. The moment the yards of paper on which the Convention was written in English, Chinese, and Tibetan were produced, the Tibetan officials simply jostled one another to affix their seals. The seal of the Dalai Lama was affixed by the venerable Ta Rimpoche, the senior Lama present.

Of this scene the inevitable photograph by flashlight was taken, or at least an attempt was made to take it. The poor Tibetans were very much startled when the flashlight fizzed off, and no doubt thought that it was some device to exterminate them all, but laughed heartily on discovering their mistake.

A few days after the signing of the Convention, all the hardships, cold and privations gone through by the Mission and Force were wiped out and forgotten, and would have been gladly undertaken again, on receipt of the kind, thoughtful, and generous telegram of congratulation from his Most Gracious Majesty the King. Telegrams from the Viceroy of India and Lord Kitchener, Commander-in-Chief in India, soon followed, which filled the men with pride and satisfaction that they were considered to have done well.

The Mission and Force remained at Lhasa till September 23, and most friendly intercourse between the Tibetans and all ranks was established.

During this time we redoubled our efforts to get sanction and complete our preparations for the contemplated Brahmaputra exploration trip. It was agreed to by the General and Colonel Younghusband, and we were to start on September 27, the day after we arrived at Chaksam Ferry; but, alas! the day after we left Lhasa a wire arrived from the Government prohibiting the venture. That morning also Colonel Younghusband took his departure for India, escorted by half the 1st Mounted Infantry. As he rode out of camp, many a hearty cheer and 'Fathie' was given in his honour by the troops. He had shared all their hardships and fights, and they now felt that they were losing a sympathetic friend and a gallant comrade.

The return march to Gyantse, having been well thought out and carefully arranged by the General and his hardworking and ever-obliging Staff, was accomplished with a minimum of fatigue to the troops. The passage of the Brahmaputra at Porte Ferry, eleven miles above Chaksam Ferry, was effected in two days, thanks to the good selection of the place and the perfect arrangements made by Captain Shepherd and his Royal Engineer officers.

The weather was fine, and hearts were light and happy, and the stretch of 155 miles between Lhasa and Gyantse was covered in eleven marching

MOUNTAIN LAKE IN SIKKIM.

days, or fourteen miles a day, which was not bad for a force accompanied by a transport menagerie of ponies, mules, yaks, donkeys, and coolies. The grim Tibetan winter made itself felt at Nangartse Jong and the Karo Là, and greeted us with twenty-one degrees of frost, which was pretty trying, as our warm clothes, and in fact all our clothes, were worn out and gone.

We arrived at Gyantse on October 5, and the General immediately made his preparations for strengthening the post, in which a garrison of 200 (afterwards reduced to fifty) of the 40th Pathans were to remain to guard and support the versatile Captain O'Connor in his new capacity of Trade Agent. Here also we said good-bye and Godspeed to the Gartok expedition, composed of Captains Rawling (Somersets), Ryder and Wood (R.E.), and Lieutenant Bailey (32nd Sikh Pioneers and 1st Mounted Infantry). Their escort was five Gurkhas of the 1st Mounted Infantry with their ponies and twelve other ponies handed over to them to ride on. We had already given twenty ponies to the 40th Pathans staying at Gyantse, who were going to mount some of their men. My poor men were now almost destitute of ponies, and thirty-five had to walk back to Chumbi, but they did not mind that, as they had had just as much practice at walking as at riding, and were equally good at both.

On October 9 the General had his farewell parade of the whole force, and they looked worthy representatives of the British army, hard as nails, healthy, fit as prize-fighters, and splendid shots, from all the best of range practice—actual contest in the field when the other fellow is firing at you. The General thought so too, and told them so in a short, appreciative, and well-put soldier's speech, which impressed and cheered the hearts of all who heard it.

On the 10th we left Gyantse for Chumbi, another 150 miles, but being in small columns only took ten marching days or fifteen miles a day. On the 17th we were caught by the first Tibetan blizzard of that year; the snow came down all that evening and all that night, and next morning at Phari we woke up to find ourselves snow-bound in nearly two feet of snow. The cold was intense, and many of the men succumbed from pneumonia and exposure. Snow-blindness was rife, a most painful infliction, nearly all the snow-spectacles having been lost or broken. The 1st Mounted Infantry, keeping up their record, suffered the hardest from this bad weather. Thirteen Gurkha Mounted Infantry had been sent with Captain Cowie and Mr. Walsh, Assistant Commissioner, to survey the Kambo Valley between Tuna and Chumbi. Here they were snowed up in four to five feet of snow, and the whole party nearly lost their lives. They only got out of it by following a drove of yaks which were instinctively finding their way to the nearest village, and ploughing a road through the snow. They had to abandon the idea of going through to Chumbi, and after three days got into Phari, where everything possible was done for them by the detachment of 40th Pathans left there as a garrison. The poor little Gurkhas were all snow-blind, and went through many days of intense suffering before they recovered.

On the 19th the snow had sufficiently abated to allow us to proceed to Gautsa. Working parties were sent ahead to clear a narrow road through the snow, and to prevent snow-blindness I made my men bandage their eyes with bits of thin cloth, or the ends of their turbans, and sitting their trusty ponies, which did not need guiding along the narrow path, they escaped without a single case. We were intended to reach Gautsa that evening, but on our arrival at Dotha about 7 P.M., five miles short of Gautsa, a message was received by the 40th Pathans and myself that Gautsa was so choked up with snow there was not room for us, and that we should stay the night at Dotha. This place I used always to consider the coldest and most inhospitable place in Tibet, and although it was eight months since we passed through, this night confirmed my belief. The waterfall was again frozen solid; there was four feet of snow everywhere except on the road, on which the mules and ponies were piqueted. No tents could be pitched. The usual cutting wind blew on this our last visit with redoubled energy.

Two sheds without sides had been built for sheep-pens and to shelter the stores; into these we all huddled together, the 40th in one, and the 1st Mounted Infantry and mule-drivers in the other.

It was so cold that even the Mussulman mule-drivers asked for the double issue of rum which the Sikhs were getting. Starting off early next morning with no regrets for Dotha, we reached Lingmathang and Chumbi early in the day. How pleased we all were to be back again in that ideal site for a hill station, if only it were in British territory, with its wealth of rose-trees, rhododendrons, and stately pine-forests, where there is unlimited room for the Government Offices of Viceroy and Lieutenant-Governor, Commander-in-Chief and Military Member of Council, and the numerous other high officials who make up the Government of India. In fact, they could each find a happy valley for himself in Chumbi, instead of being piled and crowded one on top of the other in Simla. In Chumbi there would be no shortage of water in the hot weather, as two large streams, the Amu Chu and Mu Chu, meet

THE CHUMBI VALLEY.

at New Chumbi, thenceforward united under the name of the Amu Chu, providing an unlimited supply of water and an unlimited power for the supply of electric light on the spot at little expense. Thirty miles of broad carriage-roads could be constructed, on which the fair ladies of India could drive about in smart carriages and pairs instead of being dragged about by four coolies in the uncomfortable rickshaw, which mode of conveyance detracts from the beauty and dignity of an English lady. Acres of beautiful turf now exist for tennis, football, hockey, and polo grounds at Lingmathang and in the Mu Chu Valley. In the experience of the Tibet Mission Force the Chumbi Valley proved to be a sanatorium and perfect health-resort. All this within 350 miles of Calcutta, and waiting to be linked up with the main lines in Bengal by about ninety miles of railway. What a blessing to the English people of Calcutta who cannot afford to get a breath of fresh air in the now distant and expensive Himalayan hill stations, if the Chumbi and other valleys be thrown open to them, and how they will bless Colonel Younghusband's mission to Lhasa!

To return to the Mounted Infantry. We were ordered to hand over all our ponies to the Transport Corps, which made the Sepoys very angry, as they had grown fond of their ponies, and were disgusted that after all their grooming, feeding, and care, their mounts should be condemned to carry loads. On the 25th we, now all dismounted, stepped out for India. On the 26th we crossed the Nathu Là into Sikkim, marching through deep snow on one side and deep slush and mud on the other. It was not without feelings of regret that the last look at Tibet was taken from the top of the Nathu Là. It had been the scene of many exciting moments for us, and all its hardships, cold, short commons, hard marches, exhilarating fights, and exploration trips combined to make the life for Mounted Infantry soldiers ideal.

MOUNTAINS OF TIBET FROM THE NATHU LÀ.

APPENDICES

I

GENERAL MACDONALD'S ORDERS FOR ASSAULTING GYANTSE JONG ON JULY 6.

Camp Gyantse, 5th July, 1904.

1. The Jong will be assaulted at 4 A.M. on the 6th by 3 Columns as under:

Right Column	*Centre Column*	*Left Column*
Under Capt. Johnson	Under Capt. Maclachlan	Under Major Murray
Dett. Sappers & Miners	Dett. Sappers & Miners	Dett. Sappers & Miners
1 Coy. Royal Fusiliers	1 Coy. 40th Pathans	1 Coy. 8th Gurkhas
1 Coy. 23rd Pioneers	1 Coy. 23rd Pioneers	1 Coy. 32nd Pioneers
1 7-pr. gun		
	RESERVES	
1 Coy. Royal Fusiliers 1 Coy. 23rd Pioneers	2 Cos. 40th Pathans	1 Coy. 8th Gurkhas 1 Coy. 32nd Pioneers
	CAMP GUARD	
1 Coy. 40th Pathans 1 Coy. 23rd Pioneers	2 Cos. Royal Fusiliers	1 Coy. 8th Gurkhas 1 Coy. 32nd Pioneers

The remaining troops will form reserve to Camp Guard.

2. The attacking column the first day will be relieved at dusk by the reserve and will return to Camp.

3. The reserve will relieve the attacking column at dusk the 1st day.

4. The Camp Guard will form the reserve for the attacking column at dawn the 2nd day.

5. Lieut.-Col. Campbell, 40th Pathans, will command the assaulting column 1st day.

Lieut.-Col. Hogge, 23rd Pioneers, will command the reserve the 1st day.

Lieut.-Col. Burne, 40th Pathans, will command the Camp Guard.

6. The troops for the assault and reserve will move from this camp to the positions allotted them between Gyantse Post and Palla Post at 2.30 A.M. on 6th, the Right Column leading, and should be in position to commence the assault at 4 A.M., when each column will move forward simultaneously on its objective. The remaining troops will move to new camp by Sapper Bridge.

7. Each company of attack will take six picks and two crowbars; two boxes of guncotton with fuses and detonators; one Pakal mule with water; 2 Stretchers, Signallers, and one full day's cooked rations. 1st Reserve ammunition will be with the Reserve.

8. 150 rounds of ammunition will be carried, and full water-bottles.

9. The position of the Guns and Maxims to support the attack will be:—

Two large 7-prs. and 1 small 7-pr. under Captn. Luke, R.A., with 2 Maxims 23rd Prs., on Gun Hill East of Palla.

4 Guns No. 7 M.B. under Major Fuller, R.G.A., and Maxim Royal Fusiliers and 40th Pathans, on East side of Palla.

Two Guns No. 7 M.B. under Capn. Easton, R.G.A., and 2 Guns No. 30 M.B., under Lt. Marindin, with 2 Maxims Norfolks, at the Gurkha Post.

10. The P.M.O. will make suitable medical arrangements.

11. The G.O.C. and Hd. Qrs., accompanied by Lt.-Col. Cooper, will be in Palla with party of Signallers.

12. All troops in the Assaulting Column will draw rations up to and for the 7th inst.

The assaulting column will take with them a full day's cooked rations for the 6th.

The reserve will cook their rations during the day and also their rations for the 7th.

13. The 1st Coy. Mtd. Infy. will provide ½ a Company as Camp Guard on 6th and ½ a Coy. to reconnoitre the Shigatse road, moving out at 10 A.M. and returning at 7 P.M. The ½ Coy. 3rd M.I. will reconnoitre the Lhasa road after changing camp, remaining out till dusk. The 2nd M.I. will form a reserve ready to move immediately as required, covering right flank.

During the attack one company M.I. will be in reserve each day. ½ Coy. will remain in camp and the other two ½ Cos. will reconnoitre as directed.

During the night the M.I. will form part of the Camp Guard.

14. Crowbars and Guncotton required by Cos. will be arranged for by Capt. Elliott, R.E., Field Engr., in communication with C.O.s.

15. During the operations on the morning of the sixth inst. the camp will be struck and loaded and will move back across the river by the upper bridge to the old site at 9 A.M. under Lt.-Col. Burn's orders with Major Thomas as S.O.

16. A Guard of one Coy. Royal Fusiliers will remain behind at the village in the Camp over supplies which cannot be removed on 6th, and will keep one day's rations for 7th with them. As soon as the C.S. & T.O. is able to complete the removal of supplies the company will rejoin the Main Camp.

17. The two companies 40th Pathans now occupying Tsechen Monastery will be withdrawn at 7 A.M. on the morning of the 7th and will rejoin the Main Camp.

By order,
H. A. IGGULDEN, Maj.,
C.S.O.

II

CASUALTY LIST, 1ST M.I.

MEN.

	Killed	Wounded	Died		
In action	1	16	—		
In powder explosion .	1	3	—		
Sickness	—	—	1		
Invalided	—	—	4		
	2	19	5	=	26

PONIES.

	Killed	Wounded		
In action	13	19	=	32

III

LIST OF ANIMALS CAPTURED IN ACTION AND IMPRESSED AND PAID FOR BY 1ST M.I.

Ponies, Mules, and Donkeys . . .	381
Yaks and Cattle	2,737
Sheep and Goats	4,067
Total	7,185

About 5,000 animals were paid for.

IV

SPEECH DELIVERED BY COLONEL YOUNGHUSBAND ON THE SIGNING OF THE CONVENTION, LHASA, SEPTEMBER 7TH, 1904

The Convention has been signed. We are now at peace. The misunderstandings of the past are over, and a basis has been laid for mutual good relations in future. In the Convention the British Government have been careful to avoid interfering in the smallest degree with your religion. They have annexed no part of your country. They have made no attempt to interfere in your internal affairs. They fully recognise the continued suzerainty of the Chinese Government. They have merely sought to ensure that you abide by the treaty made on your behalf by the Amban in 1890; that trade relations between India and Tibet, which are no less advantageous to you than to us, should be established as they have been with every other country in the world, except Tibet; that British representatives should be treated with respect in future; and that you should not depart from your traditional policy in regard to relations with other countries.

The treaty now made I promise, on behalf of the British Government, we will rigidly observe. But I must also warn you we will as rigidly enforce it. Any infringement will surely be punished; any obstruction to trade, any disrespect or injury to British subjects will be noticed and requirement exacted. We treat you well when you come to India. We take not a single rupee in customs duty from your merchants. We allow Tibetans to travel or reside wherever they will. We preserve the ancient buildings of the Buddhist faith. But we expect when we come to Tibet that we should be treated with no less consideration and respect than we show to you in India.

You have found us bad enemies when you have not observed treaty obligations and shown disrespect to the British Representative. You will find us equally good friends if you keep the present treaty and show civility.

I trust that the peace which has this moment been established will last for ever, and that we may never again be forced to treat you as enemies.

As a first token of peace I will ask General Macdonald to release all prisoners of war, and I shall expect that you will set at liberty all those imprisoned on account of dealings with us.

V

EXTRACT FROM THE GAZETTE OF INDIA, 11TH NOVEMBER, 1904

SPECIAL

No. 1065.—The Right Hon'ble the Viceroy and Governor General of India in Council is pleased to direct the publication of the following letter from the Adjutant-General in India, dated the 26th October 1904, forwarding a despatch from Brigadier-General J. R. L. Macdonald, C.B., R.E., Commanding Tibet Mission Escort, describing the operations of the troops which accompanied the Mission to Tibet.

2. The Governor General in Council entirely concurs

with the Commander-in-Chief in India in his appreciation of the skilful manner in which Brigadier-General Macdonald has carried out the duty entrusted to him. His Excellency in Council is also fully sensible of the excellent conduct of the officers and men engaged in the operations, which were of the most trying nature, and he has noticed with satisfaction the good service of those who have been specially brought to notice. His Excellency in Council is glad to have the opportunity of expressing his appreciation of the excellent services rendered by all ranks of the Supply and Transport Corps. The services of the late Major G. H. Bretherton, to whose untiring energy and power of organisation the successful advance of the Mission to Lhasa under exceptionally difficult conditions was largely due, calls for special notice.

The services of the Civil Officers to which allusion is made in General Macdonald's despatch will form the subject of a separate notification hereafter.

FROM MAJOR-GENERAL B. DUFF, C.B., C.I.E., ADJUTANT-GENERAL IN INDIA, TO THE SECRETARY TO THE GOVERNMENT OF INDIA, MILITARY DEPARTMENT.—(No. 2917-A., DATED SIMLA, THE 26TH OCTOBER 1904.)

I am directed by the Commander-in-Chief to forward, for the information of the Government of India, the accompanying despatch from Brigadier-General J. R. L. Macdonald, C.B., R.E., describing the operations of the troops which accompanied the Mission to Tibet.

2. It will be seen from the despatch that the work which fell to the troops had to be carried out in the face of physical difficulties which subjected them to the severest hardships and privations, and these became increasingly

acute as they neared their destination. Notwithstanding these difficulties, supplemented as they were by armed opposition, the undertaking was carried through in so successful a manner as to constitute it a highly creditable achievement. The Commander-in-Chief gladly takes this opportunity of placing on record publicly his approbation of the admirable arrangements made by Brigadier-General Macdonald and of the good services of the officers—Regimental, Staff and Departmental—and of the troops through whose efforts the objects of the Mission were so successfully attained. Not the least gratifying and creditable feature of the undertaking was the excellent discipline and conduct of the troops, as exemplified in their abstention from acts of spoliation, despite the many temptations with which they were confronted throughout the operations.

3. A list of the rewards which His Excellency recommends should be bestowed on those who specially distinguished themselves is forwarded under separate cover.

From Brigadier-General J. R. L. Macdonald, C.B., R.E., Commanding Tibet Mission Force, to the Adjutant-General in India.—(No. 1532-A., dated Gyangtse, the 9th October 1904.)

I have the honour to submit this my final despatch on the operations of the Tibet Mission Escort during 1903–04, operations which had to be carried out in the face of exceptional natural and climatic difficulties.

1. The theatre of operations was on the whole singularly barren and sterile, the only comparatively fertile districts being the Chumbi Valley, the Gyangtse-Shigatse Valley, the Sangpo Valley near Chaksam, and the Lhassa district.

The operations had to be carried out at an average

altitude of 14,000 feet, while the troops had more than once to fight at altitudes of 17,000 to 18,000 feet. Four lofty ranges had to be surmounted by passes of 14,200, 15,200, 16,600 and 16,400 feet, respectively, and the first two of these had to be regularly traversed during the winter, when gales, snow and 50 degrees of frost were not unusual.

2. The Escort had to traverse two stretches of country each nearly 100 miles, when not only food for the men, but grain, fodder and even fuel had to be transported in whole and part.

To these difficulties must be added the passage of the Sangpo, a rapid and dangerous river. In addition to the formidable natural obstacles, we had to overcome the obstinate resistance of the Tibetans, whose inferior armament and want of tactical skill were largely counterbalanced by their great superiority of numbers, by the solidity of their fortifications, and the immense natural strength of their positions.

3. The first phase of the operations included the occupation of the Chumbi Valley and the period of preparation for the advance on Gyangtse; or from 15th October 1903 to 24th March 1904. In December 1903 the enemy had collected a considerable body of troops to watch the Mission at Khamba Jong, and every effort was made to encourage them in the idea that our main advance was to be made from there. Thus when the Mission withdrew into Sikkim on the 13th December simultaneously with the main advance into the Chumbi Valley, it appears that a number of the enemy's levies, seeing the former movement, and not having time to hear of the latter, disbanded, and could not be again collected in time to

resist our advance up the Chumbi Valley. Chumbi was occupied on the 15th December 1903 and a flying column pushed on and secured Phari Jong on 20th December, thus completing our hold on the valley. For urgent political reasons the Mission was installed at Tuna on the 8th January 1904, with sufficient escort to protect them against the 2,000 to 3,000 Tibetans who had by now assembled at Guru. Between the Chumbi Valley and Gyangtse stretched a barren tract of about 100 miles where not even fuel or fodder could be depended on, and before an advance in force could be made some 15,000 maunds of supplies had to be collected at Phari. The forwarding of this mass of stores in midwinter, over the lofty passes which separate Sikkim from Chumbi, was one of immense difficulty. The Nepaulese Yaks had succumbed to various diseases, and I relied on 700 ekkas to take their place on the barren uplands of Tibet; these ekkas also had to be carried in pieces over the mountains before they could be utilised at Phari. The roads also were execrable, and their improvement when the soil was frost-bound, a work of extreme labour. This period of preparation was one of grim strain, and I cannot speak too highly of the fortitude and endurance of all ranks, by whose efforts the necessary arrangements were completed by the 24th March 1904.

4. The second phase included the advance to Gyangtse and the period of preparation for the advance on Lhassa if necessary. For though the actual decision to advance to Lhassa was not arrived at till July, the military preparations for such an eventuality had to be made in advance.

This period extended from 25th March to 12th June.

On the 29th March the Gyangtse column was concentrated at Tuna, and next day all available transport returned to Phari to bring up supplies. The Tibetans had now about 7,000 men in the field distributed as follows: 3,000 at Guru guarding the Gyangtse road, 2,000 at Hram, east of the Bamtso lake, guarding the Lhassa road, and 2,000 in reserve between Kala Tso and Gyangtse. The first-mentioned body commenced active hostilities on the 31st March as we marched to Guru, and were completely defeated. This defeat led to the hasty retirement of the Hram force on Kala Tso. A company was left at Tuna and the advance to Gyangtse was resumed on the 4th April, the enemy falling back before us, and skirmishing at Samoda and Kangma.

On the 10th April, having received reinforcements from Gyangtse, they stood at the Zamdang gorge and were again decisively beaten. Our Escort pushed on, and on the 11th April were before Gyangtse, the Fort at which place was surrendered to us next day. The Mission were then located in the village of Chungloo, which was fortified and provisioned, and Lieutenant-Colonel H. R. Brander, 32nd Pioneers, was placed in command of their escort, consisting of 500 Rifles, 50 Mounted Infantry, two seven-pounders and two Maxims with details, and with sufficient transport for a moveable column of 400 men and two guns. The remainder of the Force, consisting of 300 rifles, 100 Mounted Infantry, and two guns, with all remaining transport, began its return march to Chumbi on the 19th April, and dropped *en route* one company at Kangma and another at Kala Tso, where a company had been already left on the way up. Chumbi was reached on 27th April. The weather had been very inclement, with frequent snowstorms.

Meanwhile the Tibetans were again assembling and Lieutenant-Colonel Brander went out with his Moveable Column on the 2nd May, and on the 6th completely defeated a gathering of 3,000 men at the Karo la. Another force of 1,600 men, who had assembled at Dongtse, took the opportunity to attack the Mission Post on the early morning of the 5th May, but were beaten off with heavy loss. They, however, occupied and strengthened Gyangtse Jong. Reinforcements of 200 men including half a company of Sappers and two ten-pounder guns were sent to Gyangtse, and Lieutenant-Colonel Brander was directed not to assault the Jong but to be sufficiently active to keep the enemy's attention concentrated on Gyangtse and off our communications. He carried out his rôle admirably, and by the capture and occupation of a house, afterwards called the Gurkha Post, on the 19th May, the capture and destruction of Tagu on the 20th May, the capture and occupation of Palla on 26th May, and various minor operations, kept the enemy so busy that they only attacked Kangma on the 7th June, when they were repulsed, and made one other threat on our communications, which by that time had been strengthened. Meanwhile another period of intense strain fell on the Supply and Transport Services, as not only had the advanced troops to be supplied, but larger accumulations had to be laid in at Phari, Tuna, Kala Tso and Kangma to facilitate an advance in force to Lhassa if necessary. The weather on the upper plateau had improved, but early rains in the Teesta Valley and an outbreak of cholera (fortunately localised), handicapped the lower section of our line.

The Supply and Transport Services, however, responded nobly to the call made on them for a special effort, and by the middle of June the necessary reserve of 18,000 maunds of supplies had been collected and distributed.

5. The third phase of the operations was the advance in force to Gyangtse and thence to Lhassa, during the period from 13th June till 3rd August. As soon as the additional reinforcements asked for (1½ battalions Infantry, and 8 guns and details) arrived in Chumbi, the advance on Gyangtse began, the force moving in two columns. The first column comprised 125 Mounted Infantry, 8 guns, 1,450 infantry, 950 followers and 2,200 animals; the second consisted of 500 fighting men, 1,200 followers, and 1,800 animals, and included the supply train.

The leading column reached Kangma on the 22nd of June and was there joined by the second column next day.

The enemy had by this time collected against us a force of 16,000 men. They had several small cannon, some 30 Jingals and wall pieces, and 800 breech-loaders, while the balance were armed with matchlocks. They were distributed as follows:—At Gyangtse 8,000, at Niani holding the Kangma-Gyangtse road 800, at Niru 15 miles east of Kangma and guarding the Kangma-Ralung road 800, at Gubshi 18 miles east of Gyangtse and guarding the Lhassa road 1,200, at Tsechen guarding the Gyangtse-Shigatse road 1,200, with a support of 2,500 men at Dongtse. All these bodies held strongly fortified positions, and a further force of 1,500 was at or *en route* to the Karola, which was also fortified. Thus, though the enemy had a great numerical superiority, they were so distributed as to facilitate their being dealt with in detail.

On the 23rd June I detailed 500 infantry with two guns and 50 mounted troops to attack Niru. The enemy, however, hastily withdrew and retired for the most part over the Sela instead of to Ralung. The same day I occupied the outlet of the Zamdang Gorge with 250 men, who entrenched themselves.

On the 24th the first-named detachment rejoined and on the 25th June the march on Gyangtse was resumed, and the enemy located in a strong position at Niani, where they had been reinforced from Gyangtse. On the 26th June the enemy were driven from Niani after a sharp action in which a portion of Lieutenant-Colonel Brander's force participated, and Gyangtse was reached on the same day. I now determined to drive the enemy from their Tsechen position and so open the fertile Shigatse valley to our foraging parties, an operation which was successfully carried out on the 28th June, with surprisingly little loss, thanks to the thorough co-operation between the Artillery and Infantry.

Their defeat at Tsechen led the enemy's force at Dongtse to hastily retire on Shigatse, while some 2,000 of the enemy also deserted from Gyangtse Jong. I had moved my camp to the south bank of the Nyang Chu on the 28th, and commenced a bridge west of the town near an advanced post Lieutenant-Colonel Brander had established the same day, with a view to inducing the enemy to believe our main attack on the Jong would come from the north-west. Meanwhile the enemy sent in flags of truce, and futile negotiations followed with the Mission until noon the 5th July, when active operations were resumed. That afternoon we directed a strong demonstration against the north-west face of the enemy's defences, to confirm them in the idea that this was the direction of our main attack. Our troops pushed in and occupied some houses within 300 yards of the enemy's line, held their positions until after dark, and then having lighted piquet fires, silently withdrew to camp. At midnight the troops intended for the real attack on the south-east side of the Jong moved silently off and were in their allotted positions at 3.30 A.M. on the 6th July. The enemy had been misled by our demonstration the previous day, and when our three assaulting columns advanced against the town at 4 A.M., they effected an entrance with comparative ease, and had so strongly established themselves by the time the enemy could draw men from their north-west defences that the enemy's persistent efforts to dislodge them were completely frustrated.

Late in the afternoon the south-west curtain of the Jong was breached and the Jong carried by assault by Gurkhas and Fusiliers supported by a concentrated fire of every gun and Maxim. Though the Monastery and greater part of the town were still in their hands, the enemy fled during the night mostly towards Shigatse, and their force at Gubshi retired hastily on the Karo la.

A flying column despatched down the Shigatse valley for supplies, found both Dongtse and Penam Jong evacuated, and returned to Gyangtse with large stores of grain and meal. An advance on Lhassa was now imperative, and on the 14th July the Lhassa column consisting of 200 Mounted Infantry, 1,900 Infantry and Sappers, 8 guns and 6 Maxims with 2,000 followers and 3,900 animals carrying 23 days' rations, marched out. A garrison of 8 companies Infantry, 50 Mounted Infantry, and four guns was left to hold Gyangtse. On the 16th, after marching in daily rain, the Lhassa column reached Ralung and ascertained the Karo la (16,600 feet) was strongly fortified and held.

On the 18th July the Karo la was forced after comparatively slight resistance, the bulk of the enemy having fled during the night. The engagement was chiefly remarkable for the great altitude at which our troops had to fight (18,500 feet) and the retreat of the enemy over a glacier and snowfield.

On the 19th July Nangartse Jong was occupied without resistance, and some loss inflicted on the retiring enemy.

The weather still continued inclement, so I gave the column a day's halt and then continued the advance. Pete Jong was occupied on the 21st without resistance, and from all sources we learned the enemy were fleeing before us and devastating the already barren country. On the 24th July we crossed the Khamba la pass (16,400 feet), and reached the Sangpo (Brahmaputra), our mounted troops having that morning seized both ferries. On the 25th July we reached Chaksam ferry and the same day passed over the river a company of Mounted Infantry and 7 companies of Infantry. As our guns could effectively command the north bank of the river, our position was quite secure. To the intense regret of the force and the great loss of the service, my Chief Supply and Transport Officer, Major G. H. Bretherton, D.S.O., who had so ably superintended the onerous work of the Supply and Transport Department, was drowned while crossing the river. The passage was completed on the morning of the 31st July, and the same day the advance on Lhassa was resumed. The enemy had fortified several positions between Chaksam and Lhassa, but abandoned all of them as we approached, and the force encamped before Lhassa on the 3rd August, having encountered no resistance since the skirmish at Nangartse on the 19th July.

Posts had been established at Ralung, Nangartse, Pete Jong, Chaksam ferry and Trilung bridge, and the garrisons of those, together with convoy escorts, absorbed 70 Mounted men and 400 Infantry. As about 50 sick had also been left at posts between Gyangtse and Lhassa, the effective strength at Lhassa was reduced to 130 Mounted Infantry, 8 guns, 1,450 Infantry and Sappers, and six Maxims.

6. The fourth and last phase of the operations included the occupation of Lhassa and the withdrawal of the troops after the conclusion of the Treaty, and extended from the 4th August till the close of the operations.

The Lhassa valley is extensively cultivated, but does not produce sufficient for the requirements of Lhassa and its monasteries, and the crops were not yet ripe, so that the food question soon became critical. The Amban and the Tibetan authorities promised supplies, but all the efforts of the Mission to persuade them to act up to their promises proved of no avail, and on the 5th August the troops had only 1½ day's rations in hand. We could not expect a convoy from Gyangtse before the 29th at earliest, so I decided on strong measures, and on the 8th August moved out with 900 rifles and 6 guns against the Debung Monastery, which was said to contain 9,000 monks and have ample granaries. I selected this monastery mainly because it was the largest of the three great Lhassa monasteries which were reported to form the obstructive element in the Lhassa Councils. The monks were very obstinate, and it was not until the guns were in position and infantry had been ordered to advance that they agreed to our demands. Next day a requisition for a smaller amount was made on the Sera Monastery, and I may say that both these monasteries satisfied our requisitions in full and were paid for the supplies furnished at market rates. The demonstration against Debung also stimulated the Lhassa authorities, and induced them to bring in satisfactory supplies daily. On the 12th August we shifted our camp to the driest site we could find in the marshy environs of Lhassa, and the same day the Mission moved into the Lhalu palace with a guard of two companies of Infantry, and were spared the discomforts of camp life in almost nightly rain. Though the Tibetan authorities had withdrawn their troops from Lhassa itself, they retained them in small bodies in the neighbourhood, so constant reconnaissances had to be made. From various sources of information I reckoned that if a proportion of the monks could be induced to take the field, the Tibetans could within 24 hours assemble a force of 8,000 to 10,000 men. On the 13th August one of our reconnoitring parties surprised a camp of Tibetans and made 64 prisoners; again on the 18th August a reconnaissance up the Kyichu valley effected the dislodgement of 600 soldiers from the arsenal. The activity of these reconnoitring parties induced the Tibetan troops to withdraw 20 to 30 miles from the capital and reduced the tension.

At the beginning of August I had procured and issued for sick some Tibetan woollen cloth, and towards the end of the month my supply department bought a large quantity to be made into poncho blankets in case our departure should be delayed, as low temperatures and snow were reported on the uplands between Lhassa and Gyangtse.

By the 1st September the situation had so far improved that I allowed the troops to pay daily visits to Lhassa City and Bazar, and on the 7th September the Treaty was signed in the Pota La; small bodies of men selected from units composing the Lhassa Column were present at the interesting ceremony as a Guard of Honour.

In consultation with Colonel Younghusband it was decided that the force should withdraw on the 23rd September. By this time the post between Lhassa and Gyangtse had been stocked with two or three days' supplies for the column, and on the 9th September I sent the Sappers, with one company of infantry, the Brigade coolies and five days' supplies for the force to Chaksam, to arrange for the passage of the Sangpo. The Upper crossing, Parti, was found the more suitable, and three ferries were extemporised.

On the 23rd the Force marched from Lhassa in one column.

On the 25th Colonel Younghusband, with the bulk of his staff and a small mounted escort, left us and pushed ahead by double marches for India. On the 27th Parti ferry was reached, and so excellent were the arrangements of the Engineers that the whole force was passed over by 2 P.M. on the 29th. The Force marched from Parti to Gyangtse in two columns, leaving the former place on the 29th and 30th September and arriving at Gyangtse on the 5th and 6th October, respectively. The supply arrangements at the posts were excellent and the only discomfort was the low temperature at night, which registered 10 to 21 degrees of frost. A survey party with an escort marched independently, and did some useful work between the Sangpo and Gyangtse. From Gyangtse the escort returns to India in smaller columns and picks up the garrisons of posts *en route*.

7. In all the escort had 16 engagements and skirmishes in which we suffered loss, and the total war casualties

amounted to 202, including 23 British officers, of whom five were killed. A separate abstract of war casualties is attached.

8. The Artillery co-operated with the Infantry in a manner which did credit to their training, and I attribute the comparatively small losses we sustained in several of the more important actions to the thorough artillery support afforded to the assaulting infantry.

9. The engineering work of the escort comprised road making (170 miles), bridging, hutting, defence of posts, siege works, demolitions, and heading storming columns with explosive parties, and was carried out in a very creditable manner often under extremely trying conditions. The gallantry of the explosive parties was marked, and the work of the Engineers, Sappers and Attock boatmen at the crossing of the Sangpo river was excellent.

10. The most important work of the Supply and Transport Department was carried out in a way that justly merited the admiration of the whole force. The extraordinary difficulties this Department had to face and overcome must have been seen to be fully realised. In the unhealthy Teesta valley one form of disease after another seized the transport animals in spite of every precaution. During the winter the transport service had to be maintained over the passes in spite of intense cold and constant gales and snowstorms. On the barren uplands of Tibet there was one long sustained struggle to provide grain, fodder, and fuel. But thanks to excellent organisation and a loyal devotion to duty, the work was throughout performed in a thoroughly efficient manner.

11. The peculiar climatic and physical conditions threw an additional strain on the Medical Department. But all requirements were met and the force maintained in good

health throughout the operations. The total number of deaths and men invalided, excluding war casualties, was 411 and 671, respectively, and of these numbers 202 and 405 were more or less due to the special climatic conditions. In addition to the above 160 wounded from among our forces had to be cared for, exclusive of a large number of Tibetan wounded who also received medical attendance. That everything worked so well reflects great credit on this department.

12. The Survey Department succeeded in mapping a large extent of practically unknown country, and the geographical results are likely to be most valuable. In all some 17,000 square miles were surveyed on the inch to the mile scale, and a total of 3,000 square miles on double this scale in the neighbourhood of Chumbi, Gyangtse and Lhassa, as well as about 300 miles of route sketches, on the scale of one inch to a mile.

13. The Veterinary Department carried out its duties to my complete satisfaction, and it is largely due to the skill and resource displayed, that the casualties amongst our transport animals were so low.

14. The line of communications was a long and difficult one, from Siliguri to Gyangtse being 225 miles, and from Siliguri to Lhassa 370 miles. In all some 30 posts had to be maintained, five of which were in the unhealthy Teesta Valley, and of the remainder, seven were approximately 15,000 feet above the sea. Up to the end of the second phase, no special officer was sanctioned to command communications, but during the third and fourth phases Colonel H. Read, 4th Rajputs, was appointed to this duty, and the force strengthened by another battalion of Infantry, with two guns and 100 Mounted Infantry. Colonel Read had charge of the line from Siliguri to Ralung, a length of

nearly 260 miles, and carried out his work with ability and judgment, and to my complete satisfaction.

15. I was fortunate in my staff, and am happy to say that the conduct and discipline of the troops was throughout all that could be desired, while their patience and fortitude under privation, and their gallantry in face of the enemy, are worthy of the highest praise. The Staff and Departments carried out their work smoothly, and with the greatest efficiency. I trust that His Excellency the Commander-in-Chief in India will see fit to recommend that His Majesty the King-Emperor may be pleased to bestow on the Force some special mark of His Majesty's approval.

16. The Field postal service had many difficulties to contend with, but carried out its work satisfactorily. From Siliguri to Tuna the mails were carried by departmental agency, and thence on to Lhassa by military agency. Up to Gyangtse a daily service was maintained latterly, and between Gyangtse and Lhassa mails were carried by Mounted Infantry every three days.

17. The construction and working of the Telegraph was admirably carried out. In the first phase of the operations the line accompanied the force and was extended from Sikkim to Phari, the construction parties being exposed to the full rigour of the climate. During the second phase the line was extended to Kala Tso, and during the third phase it accompanied the force to Gyangtse. Throughout the whole operations the work of this department was thoroughly satisfactory in every way.

18. The operations threw a very great deal of extra work on the Public Works Department, both in the Teesta Valley and in Sikkim. I always found the officers of the department ready to furnish all the assistance in their power, and would wish the name of Mr. H. H. Green,

Executive Engineer, Sikkim, brought forward for special consideration for his zealous and excellent work. Mr. R. Dover, State Engineer, Sikkim, also rendered great assistance.

19. I am much indebted to the Government of Bengal for their ready assistance, and trust that the special valuable services rendered by Mr. J. H. E. Garrette, I.C.S., Deputy Commissioner of Darjeeling, may be recognised by the Government of India.

20. His Highness the Maharajah of Nepal and the Nepal Durbar offered substantial help in the matter of transport, while His Highness's Agent in Lhassa, Captain Jit Bahadur Khattri Chittri Vakil, at all times placed his valuable services at my disposal in the matter of collecting information and supplies.

I would wish to express my acknowledgment of the cordial assistance afforded by the Tongsa Penlop of Bhutan.

His Highness the Raja of Sikkim placed the resources of his State both in men and animals at our disposal, and a locally raised Cooly Corps, organised by Mr. J. C. White, Political Officer, Sikkim, worked over the Nathula pass from January till the end of the operations in a very efficient manner.

In this connection I would wish that His Excellency the Commander-in-Chief will bring to the special notice of the Government of India the names of Mr. J. C. White, and the Kumar of Sikkim, both of whom personally interested themselves in the working of the Sikkim Cooly Corps in the most inclement weather.

21. I attach list of the names of the officers and men whom I wish to bring to the notice of His Excellency the Commander-in-Chief.

ABSTRACT OF WAR CASUALTIES

Date	Place	Nature	Killed					Wounded					Total	Percentage of loss of fighting men engaged
			British Officers	British Rank and File	Native Officers	Native Rank and File	Followers	British Officers	British Rank and File	Native Officers	Native Rank and File	Followers		
January 7	Phari	Fracas	—	—	—	—	—	1	—	—	1	1	3	
March 31	Guru	Action	—	—	—	—	—	2	—	1	10	—	13	1·25 per cent.
April 7	Guru	Explosion	—	—	1	4	—	1	—	—	2	4	12	
April 10	Zamdang	Engagement	—	—	—	—	—	—	—	1	2	—	3	
April 15	Gyantse	Explosion	—	—	—	—	—	1	—	—	13	—	14	
May 5	Gyantse	Defence post	—	—	—	—	1	—	—	—	4	1	6	2·25 per cent.
May 6	Karola	Action	1	—	—	4	—	—	—	—	13	—	18	5·00 per cent.
May 12	Gyantse	Jong's fire	—	—	—	—	1	—	—	—	1	—	2	
May 19	Gyantse	Sortie	—	—	—	—	—	—	—	—	3	—	3	1·50 per cent.
May 19	Gyantse	Defence Mails	—	—	—	1	—	—	—	—	2	—	3	
May 19	Gyantse	Jong's fire	—	—	—	—	—	—	—	—	1	—	1	
May 20	Gyantse	Capture of Tagu	—	—	—	2	—	1	—	—	3	—	6	2·00 per cent.
May 26	Gyantse	Capture of Palla	1	—	—	3	—	3	—	—	9	—	16	3·70 per cent.
June 4	Gyantse	Jong's fire	—	—	—	—	—	—	—	—	1	—	1	
June 5	Gyantse	Jong's fire	—	—	—	—	—	—	—	—	1	—	1	
June 7	Kangma	Defence post	—	—	—	1	1	—	—	—	6	—	8	3·80 per cent.

ABSTRACT OF WAR CASUALIES (*continued*)

Date	Place	Nature	Killed					Wounded					Total	Percentage of loss of fighting men engaged
			British Officers	British Rank and File	Native Officers	Native Rank and File	Followers	British Officers	British Rank and File	Native Officers	Native Rank and File	Followers		
June 8	Gyantse	Jong's fire	—	—	—	1	—	—	—	—	—	—	1	
June 9	Gyantse	Jong's fire	—	—	—	—	—	—	—	—	2	—	2	
June 25	Niani	Skirmish	—	—	—	—	—	—	—	—	1	—	1	
June 26	Niani	Action	—	—	—	5	—	1	—	1	9	—	16	
June 28	Tsechen	Action	1	—	—	—	—	—	—	—	7	—	8	
July 5	Gyantse	Demonstration	—	—	—	—	—	—	—	—	1	—	1	
July 6	Gyantse	Capture of Jong	1	—	—	3	—	7	3	1	22	—	37	2·30 per cent.
July 7	Gyantse	Explosion	—	—	—	—	—	—	8	—	—	—	8	
July 12	Gyantse	Demolition	—	—	—	—	—	—	—	—	—	5	5	
July 18	Karola	Engagement	—	—	—	1	—	—	—	—	2	—	3	
July 25	Chaksam	Crossing River	1	—	—	3	—	—	—	—	—	—	4	
August 18	Lhassa	Attack by fanatic	—	—	—	—	—	2	—	—	—	—	2	
August 20	Chaksam	Crossing river	—	—	—	—	—	—	—	—	—	4	4	
		Total	5	—	1	28	3	19	11	4	116	15	202	

LONDON GAZETTE

War Office, 16th December, 1904.

The King has been graciously pleased to give orders for the following appointments to the Most Honourable Order of the Bath, in recognition of the services of the undermentioned Officers with the Tibet Mission Escort :—

To be Ordinary Members of the Military Division of the Third Class, or Companion of the said Most Honourable Order, viz. :—

Lieutenant-Colonel and Brevet-Colonel Hastings Read, Indian Army.

Lieutenant-Colonel Lawrence Augustine Waddell, M.B., C.I.E., Indian Medical Service.

Lieutenant-Colonel Edward Joshua Cooper, D.S.O., Royal Fusiliers.

Lieutenant-Colonel Arthur Fountaine-Hogge, Indian Army.

Lieutenant-Colonel Mark Ancrum Kerr, Indian Army.

Lieutenant-Colonel Herbert Ralph Brander, Indian Army.

The King has also been graciously pleased to give orders for the following appointments to the Distinguished Service Order, and promotions in the Army, in recognition of the services of the undermentioned Officers with the Tibet Mission Escort. The promotions to bear date of 10th November 1904 :—

To be Companions of the Distinguished Service Order, viz.:—

Major Alexander Mullaly, Indian Army.

Major Frank Murray, Indian Army.

Major Robert Cobb Lye, Indian Army.

Major MacCarthy Reagh Emmet Ray, Indian Army.

Captain Charles Hesketh Grant Moore, Indian Army.

Captain Thomas Mawe Luke, Royal Artillery.

Captain Julian Lawrence Fisher, Royal Fusiliers.

Captain Dashwood William Harrington Humphreys, Indian Army.

Lieutenant George Cecil Hodgson, Indian Army.

Brevet.

To be Colonel.—Lieutenant-Colonel Frederick Campbell, D.S.O., Indian Army.

To be Lieutenant-Colonels.—Captain and Brevet Major William George Lawrence Beynon, D.S.O., Indian Army.

Major Richard Woodfield Fuller, Royal Artillery.

Major Herbert Augustus Iggulden, the Sherwood Foresters (Nottinghamshire and Derbyshire Regiment).

To be Majors.—Captain Seymour Hulbert Sheppard, D.S.O., Royal Engineers.

Captain William John Ottley, Indian Army.

PRINTED BY
SPOTTISWOODE AND CO. LTD., NEW-STREET SQUARE
LONDON

